WOMEN WHO WALK WITH HORSES

Healing Through Horse Wisdom

TRACY L. GRAY

Photos: Courtney Munson @ cocos photography

ISBN: 978-1-7776186-0-5

ACKNOWLEDGMENTS

This book would not be possible if it weren't for the models, mentors and mirrors who've supported me on my journey thus far. The wise women who forged their own path and created a life by their own design. It is deeply inspiring to follow in the footsteps of such diverse feminine leadership.

Thank you Ariana Strozzi Mazzucchi, Sarah Bradley, Linda Kohanov, Marni Coulter, Lucinda Gray, Loretta Cella, Linda Ann Bowling, Dionne Paul, Julie Davidson and Allison Cannon.

DEDICATION

This book is dedicated first and foremost to the horses. Without the generosity of their wise spirit, I for one, would surely be a lost soul. This book would not be possible without the curiosity, trust and bravery of hundreds of women and children I've had the privilege of working with over the last 23 years. Last, I want to thank my children Josh and Holly, for inspiring me to transcend my own limitations and grow into the mother and human I am still becoming. I love you to the moon and back.

TABLE OF CONTENTS

PREFACE

This winter I sat on the dirt floor in a circle of 13 other women, the strangling heat of this indigenous sweat ceremony induced my pores to open, releasing a floodgate of toxins and old wounds to flow out of me and onto the earth. I reflect on where I've come from, how far I've traveled, and where I currently find myself.

I was born and raised on the beautiful Sunshine Coast of BC. The unceded territory of the Shishalh Nation. Sechelt, a land between two waters. I am a stranger to most of the women I sit with in this ceremony, yet there is a sense of knowing them and them knowing me. As we witness each other's stories, offering up prayers of gratitude and cries for help, I sense we are more similar than we are different.

As we sit together in this shared sacred circle, the liquid flows out of me and onto the earth. In the darkness, I consider my relationship with grounding and flowing. There is humility and blessings to be found in the enduring of hard things. I sit in this discomfort and welcome such gifts. For it's been the hard things that have brought about the biggest blessings in my life thus far. Maybe you feel similarly.

Wisdom can show up in the most unsuspecting places. A forest, a shoreline. A mountain top or even a saddle. It's often what we seek to avoid; discomfort, which is the very thing that shapes us into the piece of artwork we are each becoming.

It is a process of both becoming and unbecoming, simultaneously.

One of the most valuable bits of wisdom I've received to date was this - Don't believe everything you think. The mind is a fascinating entity. It can liberate, yet it can also imprison. Our minds create stories, and these stories have the power to create possibility and potential in our life. These stories also have the potential to create restriction, resistance, and ultimately destructive behavior patterns.

As I sit in the darkness and nearly unbearable heat for almost five hours, listening to the stories of my sisters, and hearing their prayers, I am reminded both of the truth and temporary nature of our stories. How they define us, how they can melt away and shapeshift over time. How they limit us and how they can also set us free.

Humans are essential highly evolved animals. We have animal brains and animal bodies. Yet, we are meaning-making creatures. Many of us are in nearly constant pursuit to make meaning out of almost everything. Consider what it is you engage in on a regular basis in order to understand and be understood. We spend our time, our precious energy and sometimes a hefty investment of our resources to further understand ourselves and each other.

If you experience the privilege of exploring and investing in your wellness and relationships, I am overjoyed for you. It is indeed a gift to possess such resources and inspiration, and to make use of it. I'm curious what you will do with this blessing? Such gifts are not bestowed upon countless women - even at this time in our collective evolution. What will YOU do with what you find on your walk with horses? I implore you to consider this as you begin your journey.

Maybe you have already explored traditional talk therapies or what's often considered 'alternative' healing modalities. Such as Chinese medicine, Indigenous traditional land-based learning, yoga, breathwork, psychedelic drugs, and other non-ordinary states of consciousness. The journey of unbecoming and becoming is as unique as we are. These pathways to healing are indeed as vast as our starry skies.

What resonates and inspires you, isn't necessarily what resonates or inspires another. Therefore, I'd like to invite you to become familiar with the state or quality of being resonant. Become attuned to your frequency and the vibration it emits and attracts. For this is an excellent source of innate wisdom that you will always have access to.

In life, we experience many challenges. I believe that we are guided towards remedies for such challenges. None of us are exempt from pain, struggle or suffering. It is simply part of the human experience. Sometimes systems and archaic value structures perpetuate suffering, injustice and inequity. Let us each become peacemakers. Learning how to right the wrongs as we experience them.

Sometimes remedies are found in the science of traditional methodologies. Other times however, remedies are discovered in the spirit of the natural world. Over the last 23 years I have counseled, educated and coached children, youth and in particular women. Over these two decades, I've witnessed that sometimes the remedies for what ails us can be discovered in far simpler places than we've been trained to think.

I'll invite you to re-evaluate what you've held as true, right and good. In this book, we'll explore how your UN-learning might draw you closer to liberation. By exploring the unique relationship between horse and human, you will witness others reconnecting to their divine sense of self.

By re-examining such beliefs and reflecting on where you're currently at, you'll soon discover what deserves to stay and what must now go.

Together we (you, me, and the horses) will touch on some common challenges, like fear and anxiety. We'll explore the stories we unconsciously perpetuate that further our wounds and ultimately create blocks or barriers to greater healing. These common areas of discontent are often a major contributor to your daily levels of stress and anxiety. They influence whether or not you feel hopeful and can maintain a sense of faith and spiritual sustenance as you navigate your daily path. How you honor the hard things, is often a determinant of whether or not you're able to live fully in the present with a sense of curiosity, compassion, and self-agency.

Together we'll explore remedies for such challenges. Alongside the wisdom of horses, we'll lean into what it feels like to shift from autopilot to more fully engaged. If along the way, you decide to rebuild what might feel fractured, or re-author a story that no longer serves you, I will walk with you every step of the way.

PART 1 –
THE CHALLENGES

Chapter 1 –
The Fallacy of Fear

"Fear defeats more people than any other one thing in the world"
– Ralph Waldo Emerson

When horses talk - Women listen.

As I walked down to feed the horses that crisp fall Cariboo morning, I felt myself begin to shiver. My thin sweatshirt, holed jeans, and nearly deceased cowboy boots were not a sufficient enough layer to keep me warm. I had underprepared for the task at hand. I approached the barn to begin loading the hay for the morning feed. I climbed up the steep steps to the hayloft, slid the feed door open, slipped on my gloves, and began to drop the seven or eight bales of hay down to feed the 50 or 60 horses we had stabled at the time.

I paused to look out at the sun rising over the strawberry mountain range, the brilliant orange and yellow tones peeking out from behind the mountainous vista. I was never tired of this sight. The stunning beauty of sunrise in wide-open spaces. The spacious hay fields occupied by that year's mare and foal herd. Their bodies speckled the fields like stars spread across the vast sky.

I took my glove off and shook it out into the hayloft, there were bits of hay and a small rock aggravating my hand.

I loaded the hay onto the ATV trailer then turned it on to warm up before dropping the bales into the large round feeders. Upon hearing the ATV start, the horses began to make their way to the fence line with gusto. Now warm from the effort of loading the hay, I pulled my glove off to unzip my sweatshirt. It was then that I noticed my engagement ring was missing its diamond. I looked at the claw setting to see it had been mangled, one of the 4 claws was missing completely.

My mind began to race. SHIT!! When had this happened? How did I not feel it?

I recall ten minutes earlier taking my glove off in the hayloft to shake out the bits of hay and rock.

The rock.

It hadn't been a rock; it had been a diamond.

I had the diamond in the palm of my hand, scratching me, irritating my touch. I'd pulled the glove off and shook it out.

I raced back up to the hayloft, opened the hay door to let in the light, and began a searching frenzy. Following any sparkle of light on a blade of dried grass. Sifting and searching through loose hay, running my hands along the tops of hay bales. I was desperate to find it.

It was hopeless. I was literally looking for a diamond in a haystack.

Hopeless turned out to be both a feeling and experience that remained with me for much of my 20's and early 30's.

This 'diamond in a haystack' moment was a fitting metaphor for my life at the time. Married with 2 kids. Living on a beautiful 300-acre ranch with over 100 horses. I was living a dream. My life resembled the sparkly shiny diamond, perched atop a weakly constructed gold foundation.

If I was honest and I rarely was at the time, I was lonely, resentful, frustrated, and deeply disconnected from myself and the people I claimed to love so dearly. Standing there, looking down at the twisted hunk of gold on my finger, I spiraled into a pool of self-pity. Swallowing past the lump in my throat while choking back the tears ready to spring from my eyes, I couldn't grasp why I was so sad, mad, defeated by this simple accident. Shit happens after all. Especially when living and working on a ranch.

Life was unpredictable. As much as we prepared for hay season, foaling season, or a sales season, life would catch us unprepared. Unknowing. Inexperienced. Arrogantly naive.

I heard the horses begin to call out then.

What started in one paddock with ten horses soon spread across all six paddocks and all 50 or so horses. They were gathered around the feeders, bodies lining the length of the fence line. Faces hanging over, all eyes on me. I felt as if in a trance, held by their energetic embrace.

I looked up from my ring finger to hear the sounds of their whinny and knickers, this chorus of longings touched me deep down in my belly. I felt the low vibration of their voices through the earth, upwards to my heart, vibrating near the back of my throat. I was comforted at that moment by the deep soulful tonality of their sound.

Their request "I see you, please feed me" resonated throughout the entirety of my body. I sat on the ATV, looked down at my mangled ring, then up at all of them. As alone and hopeless as I felt at that moment, the vibration of the herds' support comforted me. I felt seen and although there were no words, I felt heard. This otherworldly intuitive dimension of them became deeply aligned with my human spirit.

I had built my life on a fragile diamond setting. At any moment, a claw would give out and the pretty, shiny adornments would come toppling down. I knew it and the horses could feel my despair. They sensed my low, dark, morose vibration and reflected it back to me, yet there was a sense of grace and tenderness present. They were asking of me, and I was asking of them. There were no words, just energy. A desire. A deeper yearning, from both the herd and I to be fed, nurtured and supported. To be valued, cared for, seen and heard. This was their call to me, and this was also my call to them. I was unable to find this level of intimacy with humans at the time, certainly not in my marriage or on a lovely but lonely 300-acre ranch. It was horses who showed up for me in this moment as teacher and guide, that has forever impacted my life.

We've all experienced at least one moment of despair. That feeling of being in over our heads with no clear path forward. The essence of that moment was intertwined with a connection beyond my limited knowing. A sense that I was held, cared for, supported, and had all I needed to carry on and find my way. They needed from me, and I needed from them. It was the slow but steady awakening of my feminine spirit. Wounded, heavy, unfamiliar.

All lined up along the fence line, the horse's bodies were still, their voices asking, their eyes knowing. We stood together like that for…I don't know how long really. I turned the ATV back on then and got ready to unload the hay into the feeders. I knew then when I was unable or unwilling to face the truth of my life, that horses would be my allies. Many with sentient souls that are here available and willing to guide and support.

Their steady presence, their clarity of communication, their innate sense of knowing are all aspects I desired within myself. I would soon know that it's the horses who remind me again and again of what is important, what I will stand for, and what I won't. It was horses living in sync with the natural world that helped me discover it was freedom I longed for, and peace I craved within.

Freedom is the coveted prize we all seek in some way shape or form isn't it? Freedom to be yourself. Freedom to choose. Freedom to stay or go. Freedom to move or be still. Freedom to engage or disengage. Freedom to hold onto or to let go. Freedom to exist as you are, wherever you are.

The way in which a horse wholeheartedly embodies its freedom brings such inspiration, power, and joy to otherwise ordinary moments. I've yet to meet a person who isn't deeply moved or completely captivated by the swift-moving, powerful strides of a majestic horse.

Your conditioning. Your wounds. Your stories. Your energy. Your body. Your pathway to healing and recovery. These themes are woven throughout this book. They bind humans to horses for our mutual evolution. Threads that connect the essence of human nature with the sentience of equine nature.

I am the teller of this story. As you are the teller of yours. My name is Tracy, and among other things, I'm also a recovering codependent.

I'm introducing myself as they do in AA and NA meetings because those have been the places where the most honest conversations I've ever experienced or witnessed have occurred. The humility, grace, and transparency revealed by those honest with their struggles, amplifies a form of human connection not frequently seen in daily life. Wholehearted truth-telling. Next on that list would be the barn, the riding arena, and the horse pasture. Horses, whether you're aware of it are only ever truthful, congruent, and completely authentic at all times, with everyone. Their very nature makes them an ideal therapeutic ally.

Maybe you're reading this during a time of personal or familial stress, relationship conflict, or chronic anxiety. Maybe you're drawn to horses, as you've heard whispers of their miraculous powers in helping heal unresolved traumas, addictions, or maladaptive coping strategies. I suspect you know by now that without taking some form of action to address and ultimately heal, you will continue to be robbed of joy and peace and be guaranteed ongoing suffering.

Not much in life is perfect, but universal timing sure is. Now is the time for whatever small, great thing you can do to amplify love and healing. It may not be easy but consider the gifts available to you in doing the hard things. Decide to no longer waste the hard things by ignoring their presence or wishing them gone, but instead look for the gifts therein. This perspective shift can have a massive impact on addressing the resistance that can show up within. Become willing to embrace the hard things, and notice what happens when you do.

In the spirit of transparent truth-telling, here's one of the ongoing stories that continue to cause me suffering; I can be happy, free, at peace... Etcetera, when those I love (in particular my children) are happy, free, and at peace. Once they're good then I'm good. This has been a hard one for me. My ongoing struggle with codependency has been something I've managed, rather than something I've unpacked and compassionately addressed.

A dear friend reminded me recently that codependency is like watching your loved one's struggle to find solid ground amidst a raging river. I'm on the riverbank holding onto a rope. I can either jump in after them and risk drowning myself, or I can throw them the rope and patiently wait for them to grab hold of it.

This was a really useful analogy; one I often return to when codependent thoughts or behaviors reveal themselves. Codependency has tricked me into thinking that I can save them. That I have all the answers. It's built on ego and control and it leaves a legacy of distrust, anxiety, and separation in its wake. This analogy is a reminder to practice the difficult art of lovingly detaching. Keep throwing the rope, Tracy. Then watch, wait with open arms and pray for them to grab hold of it. Rinse and repeat.

This story has robbed me of joy and makes me a co-conspirator in my own suffering. I'm so tired of it. I'm ready to unpack its origin and begin to embrace telling a story that feels in sync with the kind of relationships I'd like to have with my kids in the present moment, not to mention the kind of relationship I want to have with myself. A peaceful and loving one.

Granting permission to fuck up, fix it, and then try again is the essential art to living a wildly free life.

As you embark on reading the pages and chapters in this book, know that you have free choice in how you think, feel, and behave. It really is all up to you. This can be both exhilarating and slightly de-stabilizing, I know friend.

When I finally shifted from feeling and acting like a victim and a martyr, life got really interesting. After ten years stuck in a dysfunctional relationship, I finally left my toxic marriage in order to save myself and my children. This both exhilarated and de-stabilized me. Not either-or. *Both, And.*

As a woman who's walked with horses for over 25 years, communing with them has been my personal pathway to embodied healing. Accepting, forgiving, and honoring my own divinity and that of the collective feminine is the ongoing work of remaining conscious and fully engaged with life. It's not done, there's no finish line, it's all in the daily doing.

Through exploring the wisdom of horses, you will come to know truthtelling and deep listening. Their naturally innate curiosity, willingness to trust, and repeated demonstrations of grace can feel like a beacon of light in an often-dark world. By opting to align your life with the harmony of the natural world and her cycles, you will become increasingly free to control less and create more.

The horse can be for humans what light is for diamonds.

When you walk with horses, your connection to the natural world often becomes amplified. Your body feels, your mind focuses, and your spirit enlivens. There can be a whole-body healing that can occur slowly over time, or sometimes spontaneously.

Together, we'll explore connections both to your feminine and masculine identities and the energy they engender. I'll share real-life stories and insight on the therapeutic value of horse-human bonding. We'll explore what processes of change and avenues to healing really look like. I'll invite you to pause and journal often. Allow time to explore the reflection questions offered at the end of the chapters. Make note of what comes up for you as you read. This is your journey after all. Your walk with horses.

There is hope. Where there is a will, indeed there is a way. By exploring the process of becoming more horse-like you can begin to free yourself of the conditioned or programmed responses you have unconsciously built your life upon. This invites a deeper sense of knowing within you. This homecoming of sorts can change the very focus and feel of your life.

Our increasing ability to internalize the value horses offer contributes to the rise in this evolving field of work. Especially at this particular time in history. Humans who engage in an embodiment experience with horse's report feeling connected to their inner power and focus, often with a sense of wonder and compassion. I feel it is divinely timed that horses are rising up in popularity as trusted allies in the healing of the collective consciousness.

Privilege is having the power to create what it is that you visualize. Not all of humanity experiences such possibility. Disenfranchisement, inequality and systems not yet effective at supporting diverse populations are very real limitations to the freedom, potential and possibility I speak of. For example, the single black mother, raising her three children while living in poverty. The transgendered Iranian teenager living in their Muslim community. The middle aged mentally ill Japanese housewife, living with her investment banker husband. When we exist in systems and cultures of oppression, liberation by way of manifestation isn't impossible, but it can certainly feel that way.

The first step to creating what it is you desire is simply to imagine it. To give yourself permission to dream. If you are human, then you will likely encounter thoughts or stories that arise which may dissuade you from remaining connected to that which you imagine. Do not allow the mind to easily dismiss you from your dreams. Instead, practice training the mind. Allow visualizations to appear that resemble your imagination, your dream life. Allow this to be a full body experience, one where the picture in your mind translates into the sensations you feel. This is how you begin to manifest, shape, and call in the reality of what you envision.

As we are all so different, what we dream, desire and imagine is also vastly different. In order to bring the purpose of your life to fruition, become familiar with the desires of your heart. This is *the practice of living on purpose.*

It's the practice of getting off auto-pilot and getting honest about who you are, what inspires you, what breaks your heart and then deciding to do something about it.

When we create an interactive picture in our mind's eye, we either consciously or unconsciously get to work on creating what we imagine. This process can happen on autopilot, without thoughtful insight. Or it can happen with *intention* and *mindful attention.*

For example, you could say to yourself after an uncomfortable encounter in the grocery store *"What an asshole. I for sure gonna dodge him next time I run into him"* While you picture yourself dodging the super prickly guy in the grocery store line up. If you lean in closer, you'll notice your heart harden slightly. A constriction in your core may be present. Your eyes narrow and your lips turn down. You are on unconscious autopilot. To some degree, you are attracting exactly what you are embodying in the moment. A restriction of sorts.

You could also say to yourself *"Woah, that guy seemed to be having a really rough moment. I hope whatever it is passes soon."* While you picture him, you see yourself smiling at him and feel yourself wishing him well. Grateful to be away from his energy, you hold no ill-will against him. You feel open-hearted towards him but notice boundaries around your energy naturally rising up. Here too, you are attracting more of what you are consciously creating in the moment. An opening of sorts.

By gaining clarity around that which feels misaligned, incongruent, and unsatisfying, we begin to provide ourselves opportunity to shift, heal and then grow. Starting with the small, mundane things like how to be open-hearted in the grocery store line-up is an excellent place to practice.

Personally, I think women folk are a highly resilient population. We create life, we birth life, we are often the ones managing the home, multi-tasking and making countless daily decisions. Ask any woman, the weight of the world often feels like it rests on her shoulders. As I became a mother at the delicate age of 16, I experienced first-hand the resiliency required to move beyond welfare lines and subsidized housing. The weight of the world WAS on my young, naive shoulders. It would be years before I learned how to share the load. How to invite in a diversity of connection that felt safe, supportive and beneficial to both my son and I.

When you partner soulful women with sentient horses, the results can be powerful. We have enormous potential to make manifest, that which we dream about and desire from within. Often what is missing is a suitable outlet. The space between your desires and your real everyday life, need not be something far off or unrealistic. What most women really claim to want after all is actually pretty simple. We want to give and receive love freely. We want to feel comfortable in our own skin. We want to feel like our lives and what we do with them matters. We want to make things better for ourselves, our families and our communities. We want to rest, we want to laugh, we want a lightness to our being.

When you strip it down to the bare bones, what is it YOU really want? What else would you add to that list of desires?

Let's dive in. We'll explore your story, tap into the mystery of the natural world and gain insight into the real, lived experiences of others. Who like you, are inspired to explore walking a path with horses.

First, let's look at the biggest obstacle most of us face as we embark on connecting to our true self and transforming our pain into purpose. It's none other than the dreaded foe FEAR and his trusty sidekick ANXIETY. Like your childhood pals Scooby doo and Shaggy the dog, where one goes, the other is sure to follow.

Allow yourself to get curious, suspend judgment and if you haven't already, grab a journal or notebook.

We do not learn solely from experience, after all, we learn from reflecting on our experiences. So, let's begin there, with an open-minded, open-hearted exploration.

The Biology of Fear

How is it that you define fear? What are your recurring lived experiences navigating this often erroneous taskmaster?

We all know that fear can be useful, it can save your life even. When fear is useful, this automatic deeply internalized survival mechanism kicks into gear and mobilizes you in order to get you out of imminent danger. When this animal instinct is activated, it essentially takes over. It partially shuts down the higher brain (our conscious mind) and propels the body to run, hide, fight and sometimes freeze. By the time you become fully aware of the situation, your body may already be in full response mode. Once you escape the threat, you begin to recover your internal equilibrium and gradually regain your senses. (Van Der Kolk, 2014, pg. 54)

This isn't a chapter on brain science, but it is a quick recap of what really happens to you when your fear response is activated. Knowledge is power after all. The more you know, the more you can consciously influence your own behavior and affect change on your own behalf.

Because horses are big, unpredictable, and powerful animals, they will often incite fear in a person. Their very nature can create an inner conflict for those yearning to connect, yet fearful to do so. Their sheer size, strength, and unpredictable nature can at times trigger fear, stress, and anxiety for a person. A sense of 'lacking control' can actually be an excellent opportunity to explore one's relationship with fear, safety and control. Often, they are all related. Unhelpful responses to fear often leads to controlling and anxious behaviors. These unhelpful responses can influence a person's mental and emotional health and have an impact on your global health. How well you are body, mind, and spirit.

When you have a healthy nervous system and your brain is optimally able to ascertain real versus perceived threats, your ability to navigate fear and consciously determine levels of safety is useful and adaptable.

When you've experienced traumas, suffer from PTSD, have adverse early childhood experiences, suffer from chronic anxieties and high stress, your ability to determine real versus perceived threats to your safety can be compromised.

It's the emotional brain that has first dibs on interpreting incoming information. Through sensory information (smell, sound, sight, touch, movement) your brain gathers information and rapidly sends it to the amygdala, which is your brain's interpreter. Your rational brain (the prefrontal cortex) is more refined and nuanced in making interpretations around your level of safety. Your rational brain works slightly slower than your emotional brain. This can mean; when your body reacts from an emotional place it isn't always taking into consideration things like context, time, and space. It is an automatic response to perceived danger versus a rational exploration of your actual level of safety.

It's often our thoughts that shape our feelings, which then drive our behaviors. This is the never-ending feedback loop we all exist within. We each have our own realities. If you've experienced past traumas and adverse experiences, and do not feel like you've recovered from them, they will continue to affect and influence your present-day reality.

Here is the good news, ALL experiences shape learning. Life, after all, is one big classroom.

We never stop learning. This is the gift of science and in particular neural plasticity. Evidence that your adult brain maintains the ability to reorganize itself. Hallelujah, your brain can adapt and remain flexible throughout your lifetime! Just because you've experienced wounds around disconnection and therefore have issues trusting, does not mean you're effectively doomed to reside here for the duration of your existence.

Neuroscience research shows that the only way we can really change the way we interpret, and feel is by becoming aware of our inner experience and learning how to befriend what's going on inside yourself. Being able to hover calmly and objectively over your thoughts, feelings, and emotions and then take time to respond, allows your executive brain function opportunities to reorganize, attune, and repair your automatic reactions. Essentially, it's using Mindfulness to positively influence your working memory, flexible thinking, and self-control. (Van Der Kolk, 2014, 62)

That means you can unlearn fear, just like you learned it. Your brain seeks information that provides context, it's often in the context of an experience that determines whether the fear is solidified or transformed. In order to heal, science suggests you need embodied experiences that contradict your earlier learning. If you experienced ongoing disempowerment for example, in order to truly heal from it you'd need to embody experiences that elicited a sense of real empowerment. What this does is contradicts and provides a 're-wiring' of your earlier adverse experience. If you've been living in a highly anxious state for a long period of time, you will require states of peace, where a sense of calm is felt in order to contradict your cumulative experiences of living with chronic anxiety and high stress. It is through these embodied types of experiences, where genuine transformation is possible.

Addressing fear in this way is WAY easier said than done. I made it sound short and sweet, I know it is not. A willingness to repattern and address a fear response is up there with bathing in ice-cold water, picking up the live snake your cat just brought in, or walking around naked at a nude beach...... Yikes!

We are complex, highly emotional, uniquely sensitive, and often easily traumatized beings. Coming to grips with how fear, anxiety, and stress play out in our lives is a necessary step. It's an invitation to compassionately address your block before it derails you rather than when it derails you.

If fear keeps you from speaking up, NOT saying out loud what's present in your mind, you're not alone.

When fear arises and you get a lump in your throat, your heart begins to race, or you find yourself frozen in time, despite your best effort unable to respond. I see you there, in your stuckness.

If you find yourself avoiding people, places, or situations where anxiety might rear its ugly head, I get you.

When you talk or write about your fearful experience, and you feel small, overwhelmed, hopeless, confused, or trapped by it, I know this too.

When fear shows up, do you armor up? Donning a sharp tongue, a quick condescending wit, and a tough *'don't fuck with me' outer* shell. I sure have.

When Fear shows up and then dissipates, does it leave you branded by its trademark Anxiety? If you're left with lingering anxiety, grappling with the need to control, agitated, and attempting to escape from it all, I get you sister... you are not alone in the *"stressed & anxious"* female phenomenon.

Straight-up, fear can be a real mother fucker!

It can destabilize relationships, it can misinterpret information, it can hijack your body. Fear is not your friend. It can however be your teacher.

Here's the thing - we are all afraid. We all have fear. There is no way to avoid it. We live in a fear-based culture. It's in the air we breathe and the water we drink.

Anxiety is fear. Jealousy is fear. Greed is fear. Anger is fear. Self-abuse in the form of problematic drinking & drug use is fear, overeating is fear. Controlling is fear. Fear has many faces. It shows up most often when we think we are separate from, alone, or somehow not good enough.

How you choose to navigate fear and anxiety in a culture that promotes its prosperity will determine how much joy and peace you're able to experience. It will also determine whether or not your overburdened fear response system gets the healing it yearns for. Decide for yourself, if this cycle will stop with you. If not, the likelihood of unconsciously passing your fears and anxieties onto the next generation is a truth you'll need to reconcile within yourself.

There is no way around it but through it. You can heal from fear-based living, anxiety-filled interactions, and a stressed-out existence OR you can bury yourself in domestic duties, sculpting the perfect body, overworking, overindulging, avoiding, and numbing behaviors that rob you of inner peace, simple joy and true, acceptance filled love.

I like this definition of FEAR, it feels accurate and relatable.

F.E.A.R = False Evidence Appearing Real.

This my friends is the fallacy of fear. It spreads poison to the Kool-Aid we unconsciously drink.

This is a story about a woman named Melanie. Melanie came to see me at the barn for an equine guided education session with the horses. We had been communicating back and forth and had already shared a few words about her desire to be with the horses. My curiosity was sparked. Melanie was older than I, and I wondered what longings were arising in her, that she felt called to employ horse wisdom to uncover.

That is most often what happens when an individual follows a nudge, inspiration, or resonance of sorts, it leads them to an uncovering or a realization. Such experiences can be deeply transformational for the follower.

Melanie's' Walk with Horses

Melanie arrived smiling and joyful. Basking in the beauty of the crisp, clear, sun shining day. We sat on the handmade wooden bench and connected about what brought her here, what she was curious about, and why she felt inspired to connect with the horses. Melanie smiled, clenched her hands, and played with the sleeves of her sweater.

"I feel like I've become increasingly disconnected to Joy. The light I once felt now feels dim and weighted down. I want to feel lively and enamored, more in love with my beautiful life and precious children and husband. I know I have some blocks and a lot of fear. Especially with horses actually. Which maybe is why I'm here…. When I was a young girl a close friend that I went to school with, was killed in a horseback riding accident. This girl loved horses. She rode all the time; it was the thing everyone knew about her. She was the horse-crazy girl. I admired her and adored horses. Something changed after that experience for me. Something less to do with the horses and more to do with fear in general."

We decided to explore this fear together with the horses. The agreement we made to honor safety and not push past limits was to stop walking towards a horse when the sensations in the body become too intense or uncomfortable to navigate. Otherwise, we would walk together, and test the thresholds of her capacity to be both in fear and observing it from a safe distance. We focused on every step we took and where we placed our feet. We allowed the wisdom of our bodies to guide us to a place where she felt we could pause and be still for a few minutes. She took in the three horses nearby, one walked up to us, sniffed her sweater then turned on her haunches to wander off in the opposite direction. The second horse noticed Melanie, looked up from her hay feeder, and then carried on eating. Exhaling a long loud audible sigh, inviting Melanie to respond in kind. I modeled what it looked like to shift our weight from one foot to the next, settling into the body and exhaling into the earth that was supporting this journey she was on. The third horse walked over than around Melanie, pausing to stop and drink from the automatic waterer. Melanie's gaze landed on this horse and I felt a sudden tenderness between their energetic exchange. The horse left the waterer and wandered over to stop near Melanie. She reached out and touched the horse's cheek. The mare stood, head hanging low, close enough for Melanie to see her whole face in the eye of this horse. I asked, and Melanie decided this was the horse she wanted to explore with more.

"What's her name?" Melanie asked. *"Her name is Aloe"* I replied.

"Ello" Melanie chimed; her faint accent still audible. It sounded like she was saying hello to the horse. 'Aloe' sounded very much like 'Ello' from her raspy whispered voice.

She was right up close to her fear and saying hello to it.

"I'm not even afraid. I'm ok, and feel very comfortable near Aloe" Melanie said, mostly to herself, with an underlying sense of surprise as she walked near Aloe, running her hand down her neck as I reached for the halter and lead rope. Aloe stood, still and quiet, picking up on that which Melanie was emoting.

I haltered the horse and asked Melanie if she wanted to lead her out of the barn, so she could get to know her more intimately. Melanie took the lead rope and began walking out of the barn with Aloe. The tenacity in her step became more palpable with every stride.

Melanie spent the next hour and a half, brushing, touching, talking to, and walking with Aloe. Investigating the kind of touch she liked and what she cared less for. When Aloe moved, shifting her body to stand more in the sun, Melanie shifted along with her. Deciding that following the lead of the horse was a dance she wanted to do. Melanie gushed over Aloe. Grooming her whole body, brushing her mane and tail, pausing to look her in the eye, or lean in close for a smell and a snuggle.

"Isn't she just gorgeous? I just can't get over what a beauty she is…" Melanie, pouring out praise for Aloe.

Aloe held her. She sank into the energy of receiving from Melanie. Her eyes, half-closed and dreamy, she stood for 30 minutes, emitting a frequency of stability, safety, and peace, effortlessness, and ease. Melanie drank it in. I invited Melanie to soak up the balm of Aloe's energy. To bask in her steadiness, to draw comfort from her inner peace. To allow fear to be near while continuing to direct her thoughts to watch and notice from a safe distance. It isn't always easy for women to receive. From horses or humans. I was fascinated to witness how this would unfold for Melanie, how her relationship with giving and receiving would go with Aloe.

We headed into the arena to explore more together. I prompted Melanie on how to ask the horse to go forward, how to ask her to join her, and walk onwards. Melanie asked. Aloe answered. Aloe stretched out her neck but didn't move her feet. She went as far as she wanted to go and stopped there. Melanie gave up. She stopped asking and looked over at me.

"So, what was that like for you when you gave Aloe some instructions and you en-countered resistance?" I ask Melanie.

She replies *"oooh, I have a hard time with resistance. I tend to give up. I don't want to force anything or make anyone else uncomfortable. So, I stop asking and just carry on."*

There's a pause, I wait for her to say more. *"My kids will tell me things like 'Mom, why don't you make me do this, or tell me to stop doing that'* and I don't. I just want them to be happy, and content. So, when I sense resistance, I back off. I don't carry on." Melanie was still. Staring up at Aloe, as if she was seeing her for the first time. Eyes brimming with tears, face beaming with light.

"Ok then, since you've navigated your way through some old fear already and are allowing yourself to experience differently. Let's practice navigating our way through some resistance." I suggest.

"Ok." Melanie is willing.

Together, the three of us practiced honoring the resistance, getting clear on what she wanted, what it is she was asking, and staying the course as the resistance lessened and willingness increased. Noticing what it was like for her to explore both giving and receiving. Waiting and honoring resistance, softening and receiving. After a short time, Melanie began walking around the ring with Aloe on a loose rein, turning left and then right. Speeding up and then slowing down - Aloe was with her. By her side, attuned to her movement, engaged and willingly moving forward together.

Melanie stopped, leaned in, and rested her head on Aloe's neck. Burying her face in the softness of her woolly fall coat. They stood together like that for the next while. Breathing. Sensing. Integrating. A woman, receiving the steadfast support to navigate her relationship with fear and resistance from a horse.

Here, Melanie was able to hover just above her experience, engaging all of her senses to become fully present in the moment within her environment. Befriending her fear, while receiving the support and feedback she needed helped her recreate a new relationship with fear. One that allowed her body to have an experience that deeply and viscerally contradicted the helpless-ness and collapse she'd experienced in her earlier years.

Unfortunately, the culture we exist within (North American anyway) encourages us to misinterpret fear. This fear-based culture promotes an internal level of constant distrust. Promoting a 'them' versus 'us' mentality breeds separateness, misunderstanding, and fear-based thinking. We are tar-geted consumers who can buy our way out of fear, simply by purchasing whatever it is we've been manipulated into believing we need in order to feel safe, secure, in control, enough, competent, loved.

We have become humans who are afraid of something, much of the time. We are the sickest, most medicated, most depressed, most anxious population that has ever existed.

How can you employ a spiritually sound perspective to begin transmuting fear into something more useful? First of all, it helps to understand that fear is rooted in what has been to date, the dominant culture.

The paradigm of Patriarchy. We'll explore this a little more in chapter 2.

In order to transmute fear from being fearful, to observing fear you must first recognize it within yourself, accept it for what it is, and become willing to release it. Fighting fear will not work. That is the old way. Responding to fear from a place of compassion, however, will release its grip on you.

It's a subtle, simple shift. One that empowers you to navigate fear, by first being willing to face it. It's a powerful skill set you can use for the duration of your life. It will also empower you to model navigating fear with grace and ease to those you love and care about. Actions speak louder than words anyway, right? Through connecting to your feminine essence, your innate ability to sense, feel, become curious and nurture, you hone your ability to detect fear and its root causes. Loosening the grip fear and anxiety can have on you and hijacking your experience. This is a practice. One you choose to employ moment by moment and day by day. The more you find daily opportunities to embody the essence of your own feminine energy - the less suffocating fear's grip will feel.

When you know how to remain grounded and connected to your body and observe the fear like a guest in your home, you're no longer a slave to its hold on you. The invitation is for you to rest in your inherent divinity instead. Come to know your wholeness, your innate essence, and personal truth. From here you can creatively transmute fear, stress, and anxiety into gold. Something that may bless and be of benefit.

This can be the gift of hard things. The alchemy that occurs when transformations, big or small, take shape.

When you learn how to transmute fear, you're developing the ability to transcend your current state of being. Shifting from a fear state into a state of deeper awareness is a brain process. It's also an alchemical process. By tapping into a state of BEING you're harnessing your divine inner feminine to transmute something of little value, into something of great value.

This is powerful. Magical. Sometimes I even refer to it as a baby miracle.

When everything feels different because one little (or not so little) thing shifts.

Consider Melanie and Aloe for a moment. By way of connecting with her divine feminine energies; her ability to get curious, choose collaboration, remain responsive, attune to her feeling state, Melanie transmuted the fear, stress, and anxiety she had been carrying for years into deeper awareness. One that filled her with joy, connection, trust, inner peace, and lightness within.

How did she do this exactly? She employed more of her feminine qualities. Stillness, noticing, sensing, collaboration, nurturing, feeling, responsiveness and curiosity. She navigated the complex domain of her traumatized brain, to create a visceral experience that contradicted her earlier one.

She needed nothing outside of herself in order to mindfully connect with what was already present within her. Her ability to heal and transform.

If Melanie employed more of her masculine qualities and the interaction was goal-oriented, with little consideration around her previous trauma, how do think an assertive, strategic, dominant, and controlled interaction with Aloe would have gone? Likely much different.

Here's a non-horsey, very human example of how fear can create stress, anxiety, and disconnection in human relationships.

When I first met my now-husband Darren, I often found myself agitated, anxious, and fleeing conversations around money and finances. Whenever the topic came up, I would instantly feel lightheaded, my cheeks would begin to get warm, my chest would feel tight, and I lacked the ability to articulate clearly. My bodily sensations informed me that my emotional brain had taken over. I recall feeling like a little girl about to get in trouble. The need to protect myself from these sensations was strong. Without consciously thinking, I would leave the room, or become frozen mid-conversation. If the conflict persisted, I'd make excuses, change the topic or find some avoidant tactic to get out of getting into the conversation.

Darren loves to talk, debate, tease out ideas and really dig into things. He's logical minded, focused, and highly competent. He isn't however particularly connected to his senses. He wasn't easily or quickly able to detect when I was feeling heightened, agitated, or stressed out by these conversations. On occasion committed to his goal of having it out, he'd become pushy, and I would react.

Finally, the strategies I was mindlessly employing failed to garner the avoidant results my body/mind sought, and he confronted me about it.

"Why is it that whenever we have a conversation about money, paying a bill, or how much something costs and how we're going to pay for it - you sabotage it? Why can't we just talk about this stuff, like two adults?" he inquired.

"Uh, oh, uh…" Ugh. I blanked at his inquiry. Tears began springing from my eyes, heart racing, I wrung my hands and fidgeted with my scarf. Unable to look him in the eyes, I stared down at the kitchen countertop, secretly hoping I could just melt away into the pattern of the granite.

"We can just talk about it. It's ok, I'm not upset, I just want your input. I want to know how you feel about these costs and how we can manage it together" he said in an attempt to comfort. Looking up I saw the softness in his face, felt his love and care for me, and noticed my body begin to relax. I took a long, deep breath and walked over and sat beside him.

He held my hand and put his hand on my back. Why was it so hard for me to talk to him about money, his, mine, ours? Why was I unable to remain present in these necessary adult conversations? Why did I opt for running away, allowing fear, anxiety, and stress to overtake me - powerless to interrupt the physical symptoms that hijacked me?

"I guess I'm coming to realize I have some wounds around money. I have fear around discussing finances. I've been operating under the assumption that if you don't give it any attention - it will just subside on its own. Well, it hasn't. I think that my previous marriage and being a single mom for so many years has created a sense of anxiety around money. That money and even talking about it is something to be feared or avoided, that nothing good comes from it, so best to just leave it alone, let it work itself out" I began to bravely talk it through. It felt somewhat awkward as I fumbled along. I heard myself say this out loud, for the first time. I recognized the judgments I had about myself and did what I could at the moment to practice shifting into curiosity instead.

By naming my experience I was able to take the charge out of how it was affecting me and our relationship. By slowing down, creating a connection through touch and mutual energy, I created a new experience in my relationship that contradicted many of my earlier ones. I practiced being vulnerable and transparent, I took responsibility for my stuff and communicated it as clearly as I could to my husband in the moment. Although it felt messy at the time, this created a sense of inner strength and confidence in my ability to build a loving truthful relationship. I used this hard moment to create the kind of relationship I desired with myself and my partner. Authentic, and loving.

My chest softened, my heart rate slowed, I felt the tears dry and the agitation diminish. He leaned over and hugged me. He reassured me that we would have each other's back and that he too had his own wounds and stories around money. He shared with me the time as a young man in his early twenties, he lived in his car. He'd lost his job and his relationship with his mother was so toxic that he could not bring himself to go home. He shared about how alone and powerless this had made him feel. This was an experience that had shaped him and informed an ongoing need to feel safe in relationships and responsible for his resources.

Instead of melting away into the countertop, we melted into each other. I felt seen and heard, validated, and supported. He felt more open-hearted in general and compassionate towards me. One of the greatest gifts a person can give another is the courage to be vulnerable and tell their truth. The act of employing bravery and doing something different over the comfort of remaining the same.

Knowledge is power sister.

Practice

Grab your journal and invite reflection

- What does false evidence appearing real mean to you? Can you think of a recent or longstanding example? Reflect on the consequences you experienced by believing the false evidence.

- What are your 'tells' or symptoms that indicate your emotional brain is calling the shots or has overtaken your rational brain? (lightheaded, tight chest, get wrench, tears....?)

- Give yourself permission to name your fears. [For example: Fear of being rejected, abandoned or being alone. Fear of failure or screwing up big. Fear of pain or heartache. Fear of appearing 'less than' in another's eyes. Fear of not having enough or not being enough] These are all very real fears, naming them helps take the charge out of fear and positions you to begin taking action on your own behalf.

- What could your life look like if you were able to befriend your fears and begin transmuting them into something more useful?

CHAPTER 2 –
THE STORIES

"History isn't about what happened - it's who tells the story."–Dr. Sally Roche Wagner

As a woman, I'm familiar with conversations of longings. For as long as I can remember these three have remained consistently at the top of my long-ings list: *Freedom, Horses, and a Sister.* Even as a young girl, I ached for female relationships that felt safe and honoring. I experienced confusion around what it meant to be 'feminine' from an early age and buried my feminine wounds under the achievements and activity of my comfortable masculine surroundings.

It has taken me four decades to unravel the threads that have predicated my story. The stitches that have held together my feminine wounding's, bound by generations of silence, self-abandonment, and servicing of the status quo. I have come to know that indeed it is possible to create a life free-er of suffering.

Through ongoing initiations with horses (my spirit animal) practicing therapeutic modalities of healing and cultivating the capacity to show up for an evolving sisterhood - what unfolds in these next pages is a real-life owning and sharing of stories.

Your story matters.

My story matters.

Our stories matter.

By claiming your story, owning your experiences, knowing your value, and honoring your ever-expanding beliefs, what you're really doing is culti-vating a sense of belonging to yourself.

This might not be easy, but we can do hard things. To honor what has already been, can feel contrary to your desire to move on from it. Forget about it already and try to move on. I get it. Truth is...this is where the gold is. The place where difficult stories and challenging chapters transmute into divine feminine wisdom is where power, healing, and strength resides.

I've come to know that pain and longings almost always have a purpose. That what we resist, persists and that our stories as women deeply matter.

Owning your story can provide pathways to healing it. For ourselves, our families, our communities, and ultimately our world.

As Brené Brown, researcher/storyteller exhorts "Change the **story**. When we deny our **stories**, they define us. When we **own** our **stories**, we get to write a brave new ending."

In these pages, you will find stories of horses being and humans healing, all while dancing with their not so unique fears and anxieties. The wisdom of mother nature inspires deep healing for the feminine soul. Her seasonal existence reminds us to sync our cycles. To rest or hibernate in Winter. To begin planting and preparing to grow come Spring. To play, swim and enjoy vibrant living with the warmth of Summer. To harvest and prepare come fall.

Flowers's blooming in springtime, the dynamic flow of rivers, the waves crashing on the shorelines, the snow-kissed ridges of mountain tops. A spider's web on a dewy morning. Natures' stories often mirror women's stories, we are after all, deeply connected through our natural cycles and life-giving capacities.

Stories that shape us

> *"There is no greater agony than bearing an untold story inside you...."* Maya Angelou

Stories enlighten us. They provide collective themes to explore and often create a sense of belonging that we are each invited into.

I dreamt of sisterhoods. I got herds of horses.

Surrounded by brothers and boyhoods, our driveway was littered with bike jumps, jockstraps and hockey sticks. While I privately dreamt of mysterious feminine connections.

I yearned for a joyful, stable family of my own. I experienced a traumatic divorce and moved 16 times in 25 years.

I ached for freedom, travel, and simplicity. I married a man with a special needs son and bought a heritage house to renovate.

As Stephen Colbert once said, *"I love the thing that I most wish had not happened."* My sense is many of us can relate to this sentiment.

As the oldest sister of brothers, and the teenaged mother of a son, much of my story has been focused on the raising, educating, and caretaking of males. The helper of parents—the nurturer of siblings, the young naive mother, the disempowered wife, the counselor, the coach, the wounded healer.

I've felt very alone in navigating the journey of my female soul. The story of my life depicts this truth.

The story of every female life tells such a story.

Stories of seeking safe places to confide and inquire - instead being demeaned, misguided, manipulated, rejected, or betrayed.

The deep underlying confusion around how to be seen and heard has been a constant companion since girlhood. The ongoing rejection of self in order to seek acceptance from others is an all-too-common female narrative.

Despite our shared stories, generational themes, and collective kinship; sisterhood, mothering daughters, nurturing authentic female friendships, and being the adult daughters of our mothers, are some of the biggest relational challenges we'll face in our female life.

Having a female soul in a culture constructed with the male soul in mind can be a painfully lonely existence at times.

It is here, with the tenderness of our insecurities, under the weight of our invisible burdens and tethered to old truths, that liberation for our female soul waits to be claimed.

Your story matters. Your experiences matter. What pains you and causes you suffering, matters dear friend. Whether you're white, or black, indigenous or Asian. Whether your straight, gay, trans or bi. When it comes to women seeing and supporting other women - we are the ones we've been waiting for. It is now up to us to become the kinds of women we may not have had advocating for us when we were girls.

When we are willing to explore, share and own our stories we tap into the collective power of our female truths.

One of the reasons women's stories are so important and deeply compelling is because comparatively, there have been so few of them for so long. The dominant voice throughout the ages has been the masculine one. Stories of battles lost and won, wars waged, violence inflicted. Stories of the hero's journey, plotlines focused on action and adventure, or that of the strong yet silent male archetype. Groups of men doing, achieving, attaining, conquering, crushing life on their terms.

An interesting way to measure the equity of perspectives is to look at who wins the notorious Nobel prizes. These prizes are awarded in six categories. Literature, medicine, chemistry, peace, physics and economics. One way to comprehend what is important to us as a species and how our dreams, visions, and values are being reflected back to us, can be done through considering these categories. As Elisabeth Lesser shares in her book Cassandra Speaks, as of 2018, a total of 853 men have received a Nobel prize and 51 women. 110 Nobel prizes in literature have been awarded since 1901. Only 14 of these have ever gone to women. Our world would quite likely be VERY different, dare to say better even, if women had equal value in sharing their stories.

The number of men and women alive today is roughly equal. Men hold a slight lead with 102 men for 100 women (in 2020), but males have a higher risk of dying than females, both in childhood and at adult ages, meaning that at a certain age it evens out. As women live longer generally than men, that means that our aging population, our elders, our seniors, will have a higher number of matriarchs - female heads of families and familial lines. (Ritchie, H. 2019)

Pause for a second and consider how many single women or women lead households you know than our male counterparts? The numbers suggest that the future is female. Women live longer and there are more of us, the older we get. The perspectives of women matter. Experiences told from this vantage point will be paramount in creating a more equitable future for all.

At this present time in our collective history, stories that highlight the narratives of women; stories that offer a glimpse into the feminine vantage point, that share our vast experiences of caring, nurturing, educating, encouraging, collaborating, and cultivating diverse creativities, are rising up to offset the long-standing imbalance.

The bias is found in the word itself. HISTORY. HIS-STORY. The short backstory here is that the word *history* evolved from ancient Greek. It's a verb that means "to know," (Oxford English Dictionary) The Greek word *Historia* means to inquire. The act of seeking knowledge, as well as the knowledge that arises from such inquiry. With the origin of the word "history" explained, there is still the question of who gets to decide which version of the past is right, true, and an accurate representation?

What stories would we tell and how would they be told, if they came from a HERSTORY framework versus the longstanding lens of HISTORY?

Some of the hardest earned yet deeply transformational work done is when women touch the wound of their earliest abandonment. When you come to know its origin, understand its effect, accept complicity and forgive all of it, you are free to begin re-authoring a new ending.

Historically we've existed in a male domination or patriarchal society, where race, wealth and gender have a direct and often dire impact on how your life turns out. If you're new to the term patriarchy; it's a Greek word that essentially means 'rule of the father.' A patriarchal society then consists of a male-dominated power structure throughout organized society and in individual relationships. Power is related to privilege. In a system in which men have more power than women, men have some level of privilege to which women are not entitled. (Napikoski, Linda. ThoughtCo, 202)

It's how we've existed together for centuries. The overemphasis of aggressive and amplified masculine values and energy has brought about wars, violence, ineffective political policies, and dire environmental consequences. Yet we are amidst a changing paradigm. One in which men are invited to de-armor themselves and embrace their full range of feelings, emotions, and roles. Women are stepping into their innate feminine presence, power, and authority. The proverbial pendulum is swinging, and it is now time to create the future we desire for ourselves and our children. One where regardless of race, gender, or status, there is equality.

Let's revisit the stories that shape us with a walk down memory lane, to the first story ever told. The one that has shaped the inner world of women for generations.

The first story ever told

'Now the serpent was craftier than any of the wild animals the LORD God had made. He said to the woman, "Did God really say, 'You must not eat from any tree in the garden?'"

The woman said to the serpent, "We may eat fruit from the trees in the garden, but God did say, 'You must not eat fruit from the tree that is in the middle of the garden, and you must not touch it, or you will die.'"

"You will not certainly die," the serpent said to the woman. "For God knows that when you eat from it your eyes will be opened, and you will be like God, knowing good and evil."

When the woman saw that the fruit of the tree was good for food and pleasing to the eye, and also desirable for gaining wisdom, she took some and ate it. She also gave some to her husband, who was with her, and he ate it.' (Genesis 2:4-3:24)

The story of creation. Man, the first human-made in God's perfect image, and Eve the second human. Eve created from the body of the man to be his helpmate.

The story told about Eve has been second in creation, first to sin.

Depending on your particular upbringing and exposure to Christian theology, the basic plot goes something like this: after creating Adam and Eve, God the father (no mention of the mother) places them in the garden of Eden, they are safe and well provided for. They do not know suffering or struggle; they have no needs and experience no conflict. Their existence is idyllic. They have only one rule to live by - not to eat of the tree of good and evil, by doing so they will die. As the story unfolds, a snake approaches Eve and tempts her, telling her she will not die, but in fact, her eyes will be opened, and she will become wise. Eve pauses, considers the source (a snake), what has been said, and also her own knowing. When this woman saw that the tree was a good provider of food, it was pleasant to the eyes, and that it was a tree to be desired to invite wisdom, she took the fruit, ate it, and gave also to her husband Adam who ate.

As the well-known punishment goes for Eve's disobedience, and for Adam's succumbing to his wife's temptation, they are cursed by God. The woman is cursed with painful childbirth and being subservient to her husband. The husband is cursed with constant toil. They are both cursed with old age, illness, death and exiled from the garden of Eden. It is told that from here, all of humanity essentially goes to shit. All because of Eve's curiosity and defiance and Adam's submission to her sin.

This story, told from the perspective of early man, about the essential nature of early woman highlights themes of betrayal, coercion, and broken trust. It also conveys the confusing message that when women honor their intuition, they betray men.

This story along with its accompanying coloring sheets, of a naked and ashamed Adam and Eve in a garden, is often the first introduction to indoctrination that children experience. Young children are introduced to a story about how the world was created and, in this story, the female is assigned the role of distrusting temptress, evil-doer, and offender of God's will.

If you haven't done so previously, consider for a moment the impact of such early education on the developing hearts and minds of middle childhood, children between the ages of five to ten. During these formative years, their social and emotional realms are being developed and their thinking and learning are becoming more nuanced.

Children begin showing more independence from parents and family. They start to think about the future. Understand more about their place in the world. Begin paying more attention to friendships and teamwork. Kids in this developmental spectrum also deeply want to be liked and accepted by friends, they begin to focus less on themselves and develop more concern for others. This is a highly vulnerable period of time to be exposing children to meaning-making storylines that are told through a *HIStorical* lens. One that breeds neither unity nor compassion.

Allow yourself to consider the implications of how this foundational and widely told story of creation might impact the development of children, any young girls or boys you may know. Told from the *HIStorical* perspective, the likelihood of such narratives being absorbed by a middle-aged child from their developmental framework is sure to create a sense of shame, separation, inferiority, aggression, and confusion.

Thankfully we have evolved. There are now other narratives that offer a varied perspective on this original story. Viewpoints shared by biblical scholars, female pastors, authors, spiritual teachers, and renowned educators that communicate a different message around the creation story - one that includes a more inclusive and *HERstory* perspective.

Spiritual leaders and wickedly wise women Elizabeth Lesser and Nadia Boltz both describe the creation story from a *HERstory* lens, and it sounds something like this:

Eve was awake, curious about everything, comfortable in her body, in peaceful communion with nature, enjoying an ongoing relationship with God, her home in the garden, and her partner Adam. The serpent - created by God, suggests she eats the apple. She considers it, it looks delicious and so she shares it with Adam.

On some level Eve already knows that they cannot stay in the garden of innocence forever. That they will need to grow up, take care of themselves, and take responsibility for their lives. She accepts direction from the snake, who in biblical times was revered as a symbol of wisdom. The snake understands that the 'death' God refers to when warning Adam and Eve, is not a literal death, but the death of the child self, or the unconscious self. The death of the fearful self, one who chooses the safest path, or the status-quo, therefore never fulfilling their God-given potential.

Eve, dubbed second in creation first to sin, can also be viewed as the pioneer of adulting. The temptation she succumbed to is the primary yearning of all humans. That of individualizing. To know oneself by continuously evolving. Eve chartered her own path, courageously willing to engage with the world beyond childhood. The world beyond the comfort and safety of her father's garden. It has been suggested that Eve was the original embarker of the hero's journey. Responding to an inner calling to separate from parents, test limits, discover her worth, speak her truth and claim her authenticity.

Is Eden the paradise we'd all hoped for? Living safe and protected in your father's garden for all of existence? Maybe…. But maybe not.

Another version of the 'original sin' story comes from Eastern yogic philosophies. It summates that the sin spoken of is separation, and the cure or remedy for sin or separation is unity or oneness.

Where before eating the fruit, Adam and Eve lived in complete integration, unity, and oneness, although it was unconscious. Choosing to eat of the fruit of knowledge was the birth of the mind. The mind representing the next level of evolution and awakening of human potential in Adam and Eve. Eating the fruit was the beginning of their individuation, which created a separation. Being expelled from the garden of Eden and suffering separation from each other is represented by them covering themselves. Eve's shame represents the separation from the original unity and oneness in which they had lived. This sense of separation represents pride and ego. It creates shame and superiority towards others. This separation is the original sin. Union then is the ultimate freedom from sin.

The matter of importance here is that it's often the teller of the story and their perspective that determines its relevance, meaning, and impact on our lives. It matters who tells the story. It matters why they tell the story, and it matters how the story is told. Our words shape our reality. They have the power to build up and to tear down. By being discerning, you can begin to filter which stories feel divisive and which feel unifying. When you practice using these five basic critical thinking skills: *observation, analysis, inference, communication and problem-solving,* you're focusing your masculine energy to support your feminine heart.

In many cultures throughout history and the present day, women are often the keepers of the stories. Women bring life into the world. We possess a deep inner knowing of how things really work. Eve's message to this day reminds us that we can be lost and then found. We can experience suffering and grow wise from it, and when we take personal responsibility and avoid blaming, we can connect with and trust our innate knowing.

Distrusting, manipulative, weak, powerless, ignorant, overly emotional - these are just some of the common qualities historically engendered to women through the telling of stories since the beginning of time.

Stories change, depending on who tells them.

The dictionary states that when we 'indoctrinate' what happens is we 'teach a person or group to accept a set of beliefs uncritically.' Essentially, it's the opposite of thinking critically, employing self-reflection or thoughtful consideration. It lacks communal learning for context and diversity and therefore it's often limiting and exclusive.

When we indoctrinate, we impose, we don't inquire. We accept without wonder. We assume without room for real curiosity. This system has benefited our male counterparts for centuries. It is also the old way. It is an outdated story. Like any story that is dying, a rebirth is emerging.

We all experience various forms of indoctrination during our formative years. These forms of teaching and training are often imposed through systems of influence. Your particular system of religious teaching, the school system, the medical system, the political system. Meant to aid, serve and instruct, these systems are often the unconscious culprit of deep pain and confusion for so many.

Consider what the major influencers in your early years were. What systems, organizations, or communities shaped your view of the world and your understanding of yourself? Allow yourself to revisit what early indoctrination may have looked like and felt like for you. Can you inquire with a sense of compassion? What might be needed in order to accept what was, forgive it and begin to move on? Of your early indoctrination, consider what stays and what must go.

As a young girl raised in the church, my indoctrination began early. The experience of navigating ongoing shame, smallness, and disconnection to my feminine self is not lost on me. Many women are familiar with this pattern of conditioning, this shaping of their young developing female selves.

Where did you learn about what it meant to be a woman? To develop a connection to your feminine self.

The church is where I learned about what it meant to be a woman. Church going women were the ones who modeled feminine divinity to me. This is where I learned that it was valuable to smile and not say too much, to dress and act with a high level of conservation, to be submissive, supportive, unassuming, meek, and above all obedient. This is where I began to war with my inner world, in order to find belonging in my outer one. This community is where I was instructed to find God and lose myself.

I wanted to be a good girl. Loved by God and accepted by my family. So, I did just that.

As a good Christian girl, raised with 'proper' values, and clearly assigned beliefs, I began early to believe the message that I could not trust myself, I could only trust God. What I felt, noticed, sensed, and believed to be good, simply wasn't. I was taught to abandon myself, my needs, and my desires and seek outside counsel. I was encouraged to seek out the wisdom of elders (in particular males) who were older, deemed to be much wiser, and who surely knew more about God's ways and plans for my life than I.

I felt deeply alone, confused, and with nowhere to go and no one to confide in. This belief system is where I was trained to abandon myself in order to receive God's blessings.

The indoctrination I encountered shaped my worldview on faith, life, death, love, fear, belonging, desire, and co-authored my purpose. Which for years was to be a good mother, an obedient daughter, a nurturing sister, a supportive friend, and a dutiful wife.

This training caused deep misunderstandings within my own soul. This misunderstanding led to tolerating betrayal, molestation as a girl, and an abusive relationship as a grown woman. It laid a foundation for stories that were deemed more prevalent than mine, more dominant than mine, more important than mine, and truer than mine, to be heard and valued over mine.

Divine sister, the stories we tell matter. The lens we tell them from matters. The experiences we tell about our lives shape our current reality and will affect our future reality. Ours, and our children's.

Today, because I've shared these stories with my daughter - she is free from carrying the silent weight of them. Because I've owned my stories, I am willing to forgive those who played a part in the painful chapters of them. Because I've named the wounds, and am honoring the dark, I'm free to reside more freely and peacefully in the light. Because I have an evolving connection to source, creation, to god, goddess, and the universe, I'm able to transcend my wounds and limitations and move beyond my limited human understanding.

Historically, because I was so confused for so long about where to find safety, I am learning daily how to create it for myself and model it to those I care about. Because I felt like I didn't belong in my church community as I truly was, I learned how to be a chameleon. Shapeshifting with the environment in order to blend in and fake a sense of belonging. Because I valued being good and doing right over being true and feeling brave, I lived in a constant state of fear, stress and anxiety. Because I was taught to fear God yet honour him, I feared myself and dishonoured myself. Because I hadn't yet internalized how to love without an agenda, I learned to love only with conditions.

Because you are reading these words, you will become aware of the importance of your story.

Because you have an affinity or curiosity towards horses, you are learning there is wisdom and power in mystical places. Because you have hurt and pain you're preparing to transmute, you will glean purpose in doing so. Because you care about others and the world you live in, you will be inspired to take action. Because you are tired of feeling anxious and chronically stressed, you will address its root cause and begin doing the brave work needed to feel differently.

Because you already know what doesn't work, you are now able to access clarity around what will work for you. Because you have both masculine and feminine energies at your disposal, you will be able to access the divine within and begin removing the barriers you are becoming more aware of.

My story is still unfolding. Your story is still unfolding. We are a smorgasbord of who we were, who we are, and who we are becoming. I am unbecoming, untamed, and rewilding myself. I am shedding my old skin and embodying a newer, more genuine fitting skin with every year that passes. Together, we are women reconnecting with our wild, true, loving natures.

As Walt Whitman so wisely reminds us "re-examine all you have been told at school or church or in any book, dismiss whatever insults your own soul…"

By now, I hope you're beginning to discover the roots of your feminine wounds. Maybe you're discovering that there isn't something wrong or broken or damaged within you after all. Hopefully precious sister, you're coming to realize that it might just be your training, your indoctrination, you're taming that has been the real troublemaker all along.

Let's move on to a story about divine feminine energy from the vantage point of one of the most empowered horses I have encountered over nearly 25 years of partnering with them.

Queen B

Bagheera (and her sister Aloe)

Meet Bagheera, or Queen B as she's aptly referred to.

Bagheera, the namesake of the fictional character in Rudyard Kipling's Mowgli stories in The Jungle Book, is the black panther who serves as a friend, protector, and mentor to young Mowgli.

This dapple-grey horse's journey resembles that of the wounded healer archetype. Before becoming a healer - one must heal the self-wounds. As a young mare, Bagheera spent her early years turned out onto large grazing fields with a band of eight to a dozen other horses. During this time, she acquired a wound. Wire fencing and the nature of young, wildly free horses often does not bode well.

By the time Bagheera's chapter on the ranch lands ended, and her season of training began, her injury appeared non-existent to the untrained eye. She rose quickly to the top of her new herd and adapted with ease to her surroundings. The training program and diversity of movement she was engaging in kept her body strong and her mind engaged. She jumped fences, rode dressage patterns, hacked trails, navigated obstacles, and carried vaulting kids into the competition ring.

"Queen B" as she has been deemed, is often the first horse that women notice when they walk into the barn and take a look around. They take note of her long, unruly mane, which often invokes a sense of freedom and wildness. They're captivated by her size, shape, and color. Her many shades of grey resemble a grey scaled rainbow. Dapples, spots, and light white intertwined with rich dark tones run down her legs.

Her roundness of hip and depth of chest wordlessly speaks to her innate power. It is her essence however and how you feel in her presence, that most women find captivating.

It's in the way she stands, carries herself. Comfortable in her own stillness. Needing for nothing outside of herself. When she moves, there is a purpose in it. When she rests, it's in a space she has claimed as her resting place.

Maybe it's the way she communicates. With a confident curiosity, and a palpable sense of non-attachment. Direct, clear, firm, and consistent.

Maybe it's how she is within her herd. Steady and attentive. Responsive yet relaxed. Curious and engaging. Clear and firm. A divine fusion of feminine and masculine energies at play.

I've witnessed that 'something special 'about her on many occasions. It's present in the unique way she makes people feel when they're near her. Seen, empowered, courageous, clear, inspired, accountable and often confronted.

Her very nature, her way of being creates an inner confrontation for mostly women folk. This confrontation is like looking in a mirror and seeing the qualities of an empowered female, the qualities most desired in yourself. Hers is a living, breathing embodiment of power, grace, and beauty.

While in a relationship with Bagheera, confronted by aspects of yourself that may have been forgotten, neglected, or underdeveloped, emotion is evoked. A remembering occurs. An inspiring ensues.

This is what stirs within, when in the presence of such highly attuned, socially connected sentient beings. Bagheera exists on horse time. She doesn't rush or move with excess. Her time is quarter time. Everything slows down, focus becomes amplified and one's inner often becomes clarified.

She has embodied the archetype of "wounded healer". Similar to the stories told of Chiron, the Greek mythological centaur who developed healing arts as a result of being wounded by a poison arrow in his leg. Bagheera, after being wounded in her hind leg during her adolescence, bears the scar of a wound that runs deep. Even now at 12 years old, nearly 10 years post-injury, her sensitivities remain.

She sifts the curious from the committed and engages wholly with those willing and able to meet her with a desire for congruence. The sensitivities she possesses and the energetic space she commands invokes healing for those who seek it.

When women's feminine wounds are witnessed by such a sentient soul, it's akin to a soothing balm, tenderly applied to the frequently disempowered shards of the female psyche.

Practice

Journal Reflection Questions

- What stories do you need to heal from? Where did they come from?

- Consider what the major influencers in your early years were. School system, religious community? What were you a part of that contributed to your early training and how did these systems influence you? What did they tell you about yourself that no longer feels true for you?

- What feels like an insult to your soul? How does your soul let you know you are insulted?

- What might it feel like for you to be truly seen by an empowered spirit? What might they see, and how does that make you feel?

CHAPTER 3 –
THE ORIGIN OF OUR
WOUNDING'S

*"Mothers have martyred themselves in their children's names
since the beginning of time. We have lived as if she who dis-
appears the most, loves the most. We have been conditioned
to prove our love by slowly ceasing to exist.*

*What a terrible burden for children to bear—to know that
they are the reason their mother stopped living. What a terrible burden for our daughters to bear—to know that if they
choose to become mothers, this will be their fate, too. Because if we show them that being a martyr is the highest
form of love, that is what they will become. They will feel
obligated to love as well as their mothers loved, after all.
They will believe they have permission to live only as fully
as their mothers allowed themselves to live.*

*If we keep passing down the legacy of martyrdom to our
daughters, with whom does it end? Which woman ever gets
to live? And when does the death sentence begin? At the wed-
ding altar? In the delivery room? Whose delivery room—our
children's or our own? When we call martyrdom love we
teach our children that when love begins, life ends.*

*This is why Jung suggested: There is no greater burden on a
child than the unlived life of a parent."*

— *Glennon Doyle*, Untamed

One of the most common wounds or areas where pain is present is located
in our need for connection and belonging. More often than not, individuals
seeking support in exploring a relationship with horses (therapeutically and
also in riding) are really seeking support in the area of connection. Understanding connection. Making meaningful and reciprocal connections. Work-

ing with changing connections and repairing damaged connections. We all crave a desire to belong. To ourselves, to those we choose to love, and even as guests amongst the herd.

We are all hardwired for connection. We are also all hardwired for struggle. Name one person you know who isn't currently or has not experienced a struggle in this last year? Exactly. There is not a one. As Brene Brown reminds us in her research around shame, connection and vulnerability *"You are imperfect, you are wired for struggle, but you are worthy of love and belonging."*

Connection and how we navigate it is what often determines our ability to thrive rather than merely survive. When you have connection related wounds that affect your attachment style, your ability to trust, your sense of safety, and your ability to manage your emotions - sustaining meaningful relationships can be really tricky.

Building and healing connection means risking vulnerability and employing courage. There is no way to address connection, except through connection. That's why individuals with challenges in this area, often find themselves seeking the therapeutic support of horses. Research studies conducted on veterans with PTSD, children on the autism spectrum, and those recovering from the effects of trauma, suggest that the embodiment and awareness practices employed by partnering with horses provides positive outcomes.

This vast and varied field of partnering with horses for the therapeutic value of humans is a rapidly growing art and science. One where connection building is at its very foundation.

In order to build meaningful connections with others, you must first however have a sense of connection and belonging to yourself. You cannot give, what you do not already have.

"True belonging is the spiritual practice of believing in and belonging to yourself so deeply that you can share your most authentic self with the world and find sacredness in both being a part of something and standing alone in the wilderness. True belonging doesn't require you to change who you are; it requires you to be who you are." – Brené Brown

I have lost count the number of times in a coaching session, where the horse steps away or reacts to something in the environment, and the woman makes the assumption it is about her. That she has done something, said something or thought something that has resulted in a shift of movement or energy on the part of the horse. Why do we do that? Why do we assume that when something happens, or feels different than it was, WE are the cause of it somehow? Truth is, sometimes we are, but let me tell you male clients don't do this! They respond most often by wondering what's up with the horse. It fascinates me how the world of connection and our sense of worthiness and value continues to differ so greatly between the genders.

One of the pitfalls of experiencing a lack of genuine connection with self or others is a sense of having to hustle for your worthiness. This lingering sense that you have to earn it, do something in order to get it. That it's *out there* and you're *in here*. There is a common belief that is reported from those struggling with connection wounds; I am not enough; I am not worthy of love and belonging. I have to give something up in order to get something that I want.

This is a deeply flawed yet very common thought process. We are after all feeling bodies that think, not thinking bodies that feel. When you're able to discern feeling from thinking and gain clarity around how you feel versus what you think, you're increasingly able to shift the perception that you are separate from anything. That you are less than another. That you have to grind in order to get it. That someone is withholding from you. Once this can be identified as a mindset issue rather than a feeling issue, what stands in your way from getting the connection, belonging, and love that you desire - is courage.

Your ability to be authentic with yourself and vulnerable with another is paramount. It takes practice to get comfortable being revealing. In many families, and social circles it's just not how things go. So many of us hide behind masks of achievement, accomplishments, and annual earnings to determine our value and worth. This is the old story. One where what you do determines who you are. We have shifted, we now exist in a world where how you show up, and what's paramount in your heart, is a more accurate determinant of who it is you really are.

Courage and bravery are the most beneficial tools to shift from struggling under the weight of worthiness to rising to the top of your highest, deeply connected, and loving self. Other tools that help shed the worthiness weight you may be carrying around are these: *Resourcing and Relationships.*

What resources do you have available to you? Time, money, courses, coaching, books or professional support? What relationships do you have or are you willing to invest in, that can offer you the support you need? Who can you courageously reach out to, who will not give you unsolicited advice, but will instead stand behind you, hands on your back, supporting your steps forward? We heal relationship wounds when we are in relationship. There is no way around this one but through it.

As you navigate your own connection story, what hides in your shadows? What do you NOT want to feel, acknowledge or shed light on? Those are the very places you must look first. Follow the pain, it will lead you to a purpose.

When we consider our blocks and challenges, what we're also referring to is our "shadow self." That which you reject or are unable to embrace about yourself. What do you hide from others for fear of judgment, shame, or condemnation? Is it abuse you tolerated? A painfully fractured relationship with a parent? An abortion you had. Maybe it's dishonesty you've been perpetuating or a family secret you've carried. It could be an addiction you're struggling with or the way you self-sabotage.

Whatever lies in your shadows, it will continue to fester as a contaminated wound does, until it is flushed out and allowed to heal. Healing happens in the opening. Healing often occurs naturally, when the band-aids are removed, and the wound is excavated. When light and air are invited in, stagnancy and darkness are flushed out. Opting for a vibrant open-hearted life, means no longer continuing to shut down or block your heart. Instead, it means learning how to remain open through all of it. Having boundaries yes but being willing to feel the joy and the love, and also the disappointment and sadness.

Is this painful? Sometimes yes. Is it worth it? I'd have to say, it always is.

There is a pain in the hiding, repressing, and shadow aspects of ourselves. That's why we hide it. There is liberation in the uncovering, excavating, and exposing of what we've deemed shameful or unforgivable.

As you explore your shadow self, and tap into what you've been consciously or unconsciously hiding away consider this: who would you be without the shame or hiding? How would this feel to you?

Can you create a vision of yourself where you're bravely able to hold your darkness in one hand and your light and love in another? Where there is no real separation between them? Where you can accept both as real, living aspects of your beautiful, complicated self. Where your light makes your dark less fearful, shameful, or in need of rejection?

What I rejected in myself as a woman for years, was my relationship with my own sexuality. EEK's, even as I write these words, I can feel a sense of shame rise up in me. *"What will my Dad or son think if they read this?"* My inner critic tries to keep me safe and small. Prompting me to opt for comfort versus risk rejection in truth-telling. I hid my sexual self. I had shame around it. I was confused and in denial about its effects on me and my relationships. How could I embrace and enjoy my relationship with sex when I had so much stigma still attached to it from my fundamental Christian upbringing?

How could I experience pleasure without constantly worrying about the consequences of sex? How could I enjoy sex as much as I wanted to without feeling like I had to hold back, or repress my pleasure? How could I liberate myself from the confines imposed on me in my early indoctrination so I could own what it is that I wanted and how it is that I wanted it? How could I free myself to be a fully feeling sexual being, shameless?

Rejecting this aspect of myself made me feel like an imposter in my own skin. I was an accomplice in my own separateness. I was only ever able to get so close to another before the judgment I had around my own desires ate me up, and I'd either act out or push the other away. Regardless, it left me feeling isolated and alone. Using others, while settling for cheap and shallow over deep and meaningful. The exact opposite of what sex can actually do for human beings. Don't get me wrong, for a time it was liberating to explore this aspect of myself with little commitment and a lot of creativity. I would not be able to move past the intimacy related blocks or barriers however, until I took responsibility for what lurked in my shadows. Until I could name it, accept where it came from and begin to offer myself compassion and care versus judgement and shame.

It wasn't until I shed light on my earliest wounding's around my sexuality, the stories I believed and retold as truth, that healing began to happen. Riding horses, and the creative movement that engenders in the body. Ecstatic dance and yogic bliss. Orgasms and permission to freely release that which had been held back were all contributing forces in bringing light into dark places. Putting language to that which held a silent place for so long. For naming my desires with acceptance versus hiding my desires with shame.

We learn how to be women from other women. Our shared experiences can influence our shared reality. This truth resides within you. Begin taking the experiences that cause shame or feel limiting and start the brave work of reshaping them into something that feels useful and may bring about blessings.

Mirrors, Martyrs and Mentors

I grew up watching my mother sacrifice living her life, in order to live for her family life.

Married and a mother by the age of 20 my small-town big beliefs mother, picked up the torch and blazed a trail in the footsteps of her mother.

She navigated domestic life like Durga, the fierce Hindu warrior goddess. Durga is often depicted in Hindu art with many arms, brandishing a variety of weapons and attacking the buffalo demons and other various evils. As with my mother, she has wielded many tools throughout her life. A rolling pin for baking, garden tools for harvesting crops, the wood smoker for smoking fish. She canned, she made pastry, she foraged wild foods, she slaughtered and preserved animal meat. Hers was a domestic battlefield in the eyes of her children, one she ruled.

Like her mother, my mother lived close to the land and for the love of others. Her value and her worthiness, stemming from a desire to be cherished by her husband and adored by her children. She quietly sunk into the dogma of Christianity, while fending off the desires of her spirit through dutiful obedience and ongoing isolation. She modeled trusting God over trusting self. I soaked it up like the child sponge I was.

She spoke of education, empowerment, and keeping your options open, yet lived very little of it for most of her life. This is where the unlived life of a parent influences, affects, and inhibits the life of their children.

This is why we need mirrors and mentors instead of martyrs and saints.

Women who bravely pursue their passions, who step outside of the box and create lives by their own design. Women who learn how to trust in God, themselves, and each other. *Both - And.*

A martyr absorbs all the pain, takes on the suffering, and internalizes all of the disappointment. Martyrs are statues on the outside and messy, chaotic, wearisome spirits on the inside. Martyrs choose to take on suffering over giving up what they've deemed sacred.

Hold on and suffer or let go and be free.

A mirror reflects back to you versions of yourself you have not yet fully become. A mirror will show you not only what is, but what could be. When what you've said or done, gets reflected back to you in a neutral, honest, yet inspiringly simple manner - you experience yourself differently.

Mirrors exist in all shapes and sizes, as do martyrs.

Where there is suffering, attachments, redundant patterns occurring, loneliness, isolation, there is martyrdom. Where there is freedom, grace, humility, and acceptance, there is mirroring.

Martyrdom says you can have this, but you must give that. It's built on a token economy. One in which you pay a very high price for something you're not even sure you want or need.

Martyrdom tells you what is and how it's going to be.

Martyrdom may save others short term discomfort while you all suffer long term pain.

Mirroring says I see who you are and where you're at, I will show it to you so you can decide if it feels true, right, and good. Mirroring demands nothing in return, it's built from a place of freedom and choice.

Mirroring shows you what is and inspires deeper looking.

Mirroring treats everyone the same, as free and unique beings.

A mentor who mirrors is worth far greater than a martyr who saves.

When you notice another living their life with freedom, grace, and ease, you are experiencing a moment of mentorship. When you notice holding something in, so that someone else feels better but you feel worse, you are experiencing a moment of martyrdom.

Mentoring is choosing from whom you want to learn and have an idea of why that is.

Martyring is not choosing at all; it's accepting what you have as good enough and carrying on.

The world needs mirrors and mentors, what the world does not need, is any more god damn martyrs.

Over the last 23 years of coaching and mentoring children and youth, there is one thing that has stood out for me as crucial in the mentorship of our younger generations. Riding and horsemanship should be pure joy. Something to look back on and remember fondly. Let's face it, there are enough things in life to cause tears and anxiety; riding should not be among them. Inherently horses will indeed provide young people challenges to navigate and fears to overcome. Riding a horse not suited to their skill level or pairing a horse with a human not capable of attuning to their unique sensitivities is an accident waiting to happen.

A competent mentor will have both human and horse's best interests in mind.

Separation versus Inclusion

A story that you might bump against as you navigate your healing path and shift from martyr to mirror, is an oldie but goodie. A common fear that may haunt and linger just below your level of consciousness.

It's the storyline that plays quietly in the background, the one that gently or not so gently whispers to you *"the freedom and peace you desire is near, but it may cost you your belonging."*

You can put up those boundaries in relation to your mother, she might hurt herself by it, she might act out, distance herself, or attempt to emotionally hijack your relationship.

You can ask your partner to support you in your cup filling passion project. You'd be overjoyed if he got onboard with ease, you also may have to fight for it and there's a seed of concern around how that could play out.

You can follow through and set those limits with your son. You know it's not good for him and he might hate you for it now, but you're playing the long game in the parenting arena. You're not sure you have the backing you need to hold tight to your position. You sense others may give in or cave, leaving you out in the parenting cold.

You can decide that indeed, that friendship isn't serving you any longer. You have outgrown it. It does not feel satisfying, you tend to feel drained and depleted when spending time together. You know you need to create space and separate from this friendship. Yikes, even thinking this creates tightness in your chest and fearful thoughts begin to rise to the surface.

Like most outdated storylines that dangle something juicy in front of you while holding something you crave just out of reach or behind your back, this *either/or* storyline needn't be the only templates we write our scripts on. We are amidst a shift where the value of inclusion by far outweighs the value of separation. Separation is the mindset of fear and scarcity. Inclusion is the mindset of unity and love.

The old school commonplace storylines that claim you can *either* experience THIS *or* you can experience THAT.

You can have the guy, but you gotta give up the goals.
You can travel for work or you can enjoy domestic life.
You can earn big bucks, or you can have a big family.
You can dream and create, or you can stay home and get shit done.
You can ride the horse into a competition, or you can enjoy a connection with him on the ground.

You can create more time for yourself or you can accept your human limitations.

It's noticing when the *either/or* versus both/*and* mindset shows up for you.

Here are a few *both/and* types conversations I've witnessed with clients recently.

- You can care deeply about your family of origin and decide to interact with them only when it feels good for you

- You cannot want to ride that horse this week and still experience connection partnering with her on the ground.

- You can feel drawn to or curious about someone you're attracted to and not yet want to be touched.

- You can miss them, but still want to be alone

- You can sleep in, rest, and relax and still feel totally accomplished in your day

- You cannot say what you want to say and still feel good about honoring yourself through the interaction

- You can want to parent with your partner and yet not want to be married to them anymore

They're all connected to similar themes, ones that suggest you can want what you want, freedom, flexibility and a sense of peace but it may cost you in the belonging department. Here's the truth around that old tale, it doesn't actually cost you your belonging. What it does, however, is put a price tag on the belonging of others. What price are you willing to pay in order to keep your current perception of belonging? Often the perception needs to shift, not the actually belonging.

Once you internalize that you belong to you, that your story is your own, and that the ending is yours and yours alone to create, you can call bullshit on this old bogus storyline. Once you know that it's you that gives you permission to be you, exactly as you are (warts and all) there is nowhere you don't belong. Especially at home with yourself.

What this may cost you isn't your belonging, but it may cost the belonging of others.

You will be a free human, one who belongs to herself first and foremost. Not a martyr, but a mirror and mentor. From this place, you'll choose who rides in the boat of true belonging with you. Some may jump overboard themselves, saving you the burden of tossing them out of your life raft. Others may be half in or half out of the boat, making it difficult for both them and you. Still, others may say they want to ride in the boat of true belonging, but they don't have a life jacket, they want yours or your kids. The price of having them in your boat makes you a martyr. These are the hardest ones to navigate.

Know this, it's their choice if they sink or swim just like it's your choice if you do. They can ride in your boat - but they cannot sink it. They could even swim alongside you for a time, but they cannot drag you down.

You are the fiercely loving captain of this ship; you are charting your path. Leading the way towards your version of freedom and belonging means having the courage to cut ties or create boundaries with those who aren't committed enough yet to make the journey themselves.

Your sense of peace, freedom, and belonging will depend on it.

Truth be told I was terrified to do this in my own life. I was a martyr to the umpteenth degree. I once got a psychic reading where a channel called in my guides and spoke to me with my guides present. There were eleven guides present, eight of them appeared as nuns - a representation of the martyr archetype I carried deep within my psyche. I would fall on the sword and suffer for everyone. I was operating from the belief that I was strong therefore I could help save others even though they didn't seem too terribly interested in saving themselves. My ex-husband in his addiction, my son in his silent suffering, my mother in healing her trauma, my girlfriend in her eating disorder.

I desperately craved freedom from this deeply held belief pattern. I was also completely terrified that speaking my truth and maintaining some self-loving boundaries, it would result in me being alone. Losing the very people, I cared so much about.

As Glennon Doyle offers in her memoir "Love Warrior," "We must do what we need to do. Those who disapprove will either come around or stop coming around. Either way, lovely."

I had traded my authenticity for being liked and accepted by some of the people I cared about the most and it had cost me. I experienced anxiety, apathy, struggled with unhealthy behavior patterns, harbored rage, blamed others, carried around resentment, and navigated inexplicable grief.

I paid a high price. I continued paying this price until I had a breakdown, which ended up being a breakthrough. As often happens, we land at the proverbial bottom. Humbled and broken open. Ready and finally willing to embrace the hard instead of running from it. It's here in these messy, complex moments, faced with a choice to sink or swim. Rise or die, live or leave it alone, that we accept the pain and begin transmuting it into something of real value. A diamond after all is just a lump of coal that did well under pressure.

Practice

Self-Reflections to Journal

- What would it be like for you to hold both your light and dark simultaneously?

- Is there something you need to accept or forgive within yourself or another, in order to experience greater peace around your darkness?

- What is your relationship like with freedom and belonging? How do you define it? Do you experience it sometimes, all the time, never?

- Have you bartered your mental health, compromised your physical well-being, or dismissed your emotional stability in order to obtain a sense of belonging? If so, consider why and with whom?

PART 2 –
THE REMEDIES

CHAPTER 4 –
THE REMEDY OF
FACING YOUR FEARS

*"It may be that when we no longer know what to do, we
have come to our real work. And that when we no longer
know which way to go, we have begun our real journey"*
– Wendell Berry

As we shift from bravely exploring our challenges to welcoming in the remedies, consider this sentiment: You need not seek for healing - simply identify and become willing to remove the blocks and barriers that inhibit healing from occurring naturally.

What would it be like for you to shift from a place of hustling for healing to inviting healing to occur in its own time and in its own unique way? One of the lessons horses continue to bestow is that of horse time. Horse time is essentially quarter time. Slow things down, begin to notice the space between. This is where we become familiar with the experience of peace and ease within our body instead of angst and expectation.

I have to tell you, friend, this one is a real struggle for me. My nickname growing up was Racy Tracy. I was a fast mover. I took action and made decisions. I was impulsive. I wasted no time and got a ton of shit done. What was a real challenge, was the pausing and noticing. Attuning to what was happening around me. Noticing where I was and why. I was anxious about wasting my time, being left out or left behind. A classic case of **FOMO** (fear of missing out). I thought life was short so best get on with it already. The problem with this mindset is that it results in a reaction-oriented state of being. There was little thought or feeling and a lot of moving and doing.

I began to address this head-on during my yoga teacher training(s). I began to get clear on why I felt this way. Why my mind was choosing to continue to operate in this fashion when I was repeatedly presented with evidence from my body, that it wasn't all that useful anymore. At some point, when we are able to be still enough, for long enough the knowing shows up.

It has taken me years to be able to be still. Literally decades. Driven by my masculine identity (thinking, strategizing, organizing, achieving, doing...

etc.) I had egoic attachments that lingered long after they were useful. You may feel similarly. If so, do not be discouraged. Start slowly and build from there. Consider what resources and relationships can support you here. Rome wasn't built in a day, neither will the desires of your heart.

The remedy of horse time became the medicine I needed to explore this experience of myself more mindfully. The slightly slower pace. The space between the thoughts. The flow of my breath and the natural shifting of energy. All of this became a meditation in motion of sorts. As I became intimately aware of this as a barrier within, I was then able to begin allowing healing to occur naturally. It turned out that the gift of horse time would be a medicine my spirit desperately needed. I didn't need to seek it out, I simply needed to surrender to its presence and power in my life. By participating in this process, I have gained peace and diminished anxiety. I have become more relaxed and confident, less agitated and insecure.

In part two of this book, we'll explore some common remedies to the challenges we face. We'll shift from focussing on what has been or what it is, to what I sometimes call 'Solution-Oriented Living'. Meaning, we begin to get clear on how we want to feel. The kinds of interactions and relationships we desire. How we'd like to spend our time and what feels truly nurturing and divine. We'll gain traction and momentum in creating a life that feels aligned to you. I'll introduce you to a simple 5 step process facilitated by the horses, that will help you get clear while remaining kind.

From Beasts of Burden to Horses as Healers

How do you experience both freedom and belonging? Authenticity and safety. Love and loss. There is innate stress that arises in humans when navigating this path. At some point, we all face pain and heartbreak. Overcome disappointments and face rejection.

What I have come to admire deeply about the way of the horse, is their innate mastery at opting for healing over holding on.

Have you ever witnessed a horse do any of these elemental behaviors; exhale, twitch its muzzles, shake, roll, buck, fart, yawn, urinate/defecate? These common, daily behaviors are effective ways to rid themselves of toxins, waste, accumulated energy, stress, or the energy absorbed by being in contact with others (other horses and other humans).

Can you recall an occasion when you spent time with someone, and you felt like you needed to have a shower afterward? Or maybe you felt unusually sad or tired after an interaction together. Maybe your experience with them left a visceral skim coat of energy around you. One you just unconsciously absorb and carry around.

Horses don't do that. They are living, breathing, socially/emotionally attuned animals. They are highly relational examples of how to choose health over holding on. How to really live in the present moment and honor authenticity over conformity.

They are MASTERFUL at shaking things off. They know when and how to rid themselves of toxins and waste, when they're not successful, they try again. They easily release stress and anxiety when they experience it. They consistently regulate their nervous system with both rest and rapid movement. They release a buildup of energy when they feel it, not always when it's convenient for others. They honor themselves and their herd mates by opting for health over holding on. From birth until death, this is their desired way.

One of the most valuable insights horses provide humans, is the opportunity to simply observe their daily life. Their communication, their connection seeking, their boundary setting, their processing. The always clear, mostly kind, and totally consistent way they are in the world.

This very way of being honors authenticity, clear communication, and conservation of energy or effective energy use - over our human way of being which often reflects the exact opposite. All too often you deplete your precious energy source. You trade acceptance and belonging for your authenticity. Maybe you've come to believe that your emotional safety is in the hands of others, instead of your own. That to employ courage and risk vulnerability, could break you beyond repair.

The dance between holding on and letting go plays out time again in a myriad of ways in the natural world. The mating cycle, birth cycle, weaning cycle, maturation cycle, death cycle, and rebirth. On and on we go. Women's lives are depicted in circles. We gather in circles; our nature is cyclical. As Dianne Mariechild states *"A woman is a full circle. Within her is the power to create, nurture and transform."*

Birth, life, death, rebirth.

I admire the way in which Clarrissa Pinoka Estes from her cherished book 'Woman who dances with wolves' depicts this process.

"Sometimes the one who is running from the Life/Death/Life nature insists on thinking of love as a boon only. Yet love in its fullest form is a series of deaths and rebirths. We let go of one phase, one aspect of love, and enter another. Passion dies and is brought back. Pain is chased away and surfaces another time. To love means to embrace and at the same time to withstand many endings, and many many beginnings- all in the same relationship."

In an earlier life, I co-owned a 300-acre 120 head horse ranch. I married into this lifestyle, and although the marriage was wrought with difficulty and challenge from the outset, the lifestyle spoke to my soul.

The wide-open space. The mountain range hanging over the forested ridgeline, unfolding down to the expansive pastures. The rolling hay fields, speckled with horses of all shapes, sizes, and colors. The chatty creek come spring overflowing its banks and flooding the grassy embankment.

All of life happened profoundly here. Birth, life, death, and rebirth.

When young horses are weaned from their mothers, they become enveloped in an aspect of this process. They know only of their young carefree life; innocent, playful, safe, well cared for, supported. Once weaned, within mere hours and days, they complete one phase of this process.

Back on the ranch, this would occur every year foals were born. At some inevitable point, the group of mothers/broodmares begin the natural process of separating from their young. Some more than others would demonstrate signs and provide cues that weaning is near. They begin to allow their young to nurse less, they ignore behaviors they would normally admonish. They allow a much greater distance between themselves and their young with a sense of maternal relaxation.

I witnessed this intimate process of life, death, rebirth over and over again, year after year. It was both heartbreaking and inspiring. October would bring with it cold winds, half-naked trees, empty fields, and a feeling of impending longing. The horses become docile. Conserving their energy during winter, we'd often find them huddled around the hay feeders, shielding each other from the cold while grazing together from the large open round bale feeders. Either eating or resting inside the large open communal shelters, heads low, belly's soft, resting one hip then shifting before resting on the other. Seeking refuge from the elements, together creating warmth and silent solidarity.

The ranch was a highly functional equine property; it was designed with horses in mind. With several large winter paddocks, shelters, a large 10 stall barn with individual runs, and a spacious group paddock. This time of year, a highly charged process was unfolding. The broodmares (horses that had babies that year) would all congregate along the fence, calling to their newly weaned young. The foals, now nearly a year old, were just across the way from their mothers. Able to see them, and hear them, but not able to touch them.

The mares, hearing the distressed calls of their confused young, were powerless to ease each other's anxieties. During the weaning process, some mares expressed very few visible signs of stress.

They'd simply walk away, return to their band of horses, and carry on. Often, these were the older broodmares. The ones who'd had foals before. The mares who'd experienced the birth, life, death (weaning), and rebirth of themselves and their young, in previous foaling years.

Other mares, however, would exhibit severe signs of stress. They'd stop eating, pace the fence line back and forth for hours, wearing a visible path in the ground from their pacing. Some would weave their heads/necks in a figure-eight formation, a rigorous rocking back and forth for hours on end in an attempt to regulate their energy and self soothe. They would eat/drink and rest very little and would constantly move their feet while calling out to their young. Whinnying until they received a response, ensuring their safety, and confirming their location. This response would provide them a brief moment of comfort, a pause from the intensity of their experience.

The foals were all weaned together in a large paddock, just across from the mares' field near the barn. They could see each other - but there was space and fencing between them. These newly weaned foals would race around their paddock bucking and kicking out. They'd challenge their container, by pushing against the fence rails, scanning the fence line for potential weak spots where they could attempt to crawl under, jump over or break through. With their fight, flight response activated this fledgling band of baby horses was on a perpetual state of high alert. Some of the foals would return to the hay feeders, succumbing to the fatigue of calling out and pacing. Finding comfort in the act of grazing, and solidarity in the companionship of their shared experience. Others would spend hours grooming each other, the touch of muzzle to mane providing a soothing, familiar sensation of comfort. Others would race around the paddock, frantically calling, seeking, confused by their inability to access the safety of their mothers.

Sometimes this process would last a few hours, often it would draw out over a few days. On occasion, it would last a week or longer. The energetic vibration at the ranch during this time of year was a complex one. There was palpable angst, a low-lying aroma of morose, and a subtle hint of newly found freedom.

This was a death process.

The experience of safety, belonging and connection within the herd had been the only experience the foals had known to date. Life would look much different for them from this point onwards. Now, their domestication and training would begin. They would soon experience being haltered, practice giving, or softening to pressure by being led around with a lead rope. They'd have their hooves trimmed and be given oral deworming agents and vaccinations. They'd be brushed, touched, and handled in order to create new bonds, and develop trust. This rebirth would cultivate in them the development of their own sense of safety with the world. Now separate from the protection and influence of their mothers, these foals were embarking on a whole new world. One where for a time, they had access only to each other, and the humans who owned or cared for them.

This was their rebirth process.

Their indoctrination into the ways of the human world had begun. Sometimes this process was smooth, for some, however, it was traumatic.

The experience of being separated from, whether human or horse, can be a stress-filled one. We have a shared inherent need for safety, belonging, connection, freedom, and authentic expression. What happens to humans, as well as horses when threatened with such separation can be deeply impactful. Both in the short term and in the long run. These experiences and how they play out, shape one's ability to trust.

There is no way around it but through it, however. All young at some point must separate from their mothers/parental figure - and find their own way in the world. It might not be easy, but it doesn't need to be traumatic.

One fall morning, four days after the weaning had occurred, I wandered down to the mares and foals pen to check in and see how they were doing and spend some time connecting with them.

I was concerned about one mare/foal pair in particular. Dyna was an older mare, but this was her first foal and likely her last. Her birth wasn't easy, she'd lost weight during the first few months of her foals' life and had to be kept in the barn in order to maintain her unique feed protocols. She was now looking much healthier. Ten months after having her foal, she appeared quite like herself again. I had concerns that the weaning process would take a toll on her wellbeing and she may not recover from it quite as quickly as her fellow broodmares. Dyna had impeccable breeding, highly desirable bloodlines in the Quarter Horse pedigree. She had a soft sorrel coat with a flaxen mane and an equally golden tail. She was a beauty. She was also our most anxious mare. Reacting to various medications over the years, losing weight easily, and becoming panic-stricken for a time, when herd dynamics would change. Hers was a highly sensitive existence.

As I approached the paddocks with my own kids in tow, my 10-year-old son ran off to do the chicken chores and my 2-year-old daughter tagged alongside me. I saw the mare standing at the fence line, staring into the weanling paddock not far off. Dyna's fellow broodmares had all wandered off to graze in the frostbitten fields, searching for green shoots forgotten beneath the taller strands of summer scorched dried grass. There she was, alone at the fence line. Standing, watching, waiting, wondering....

I glanced over to the weanling's pen, there were eight in total this year. Only two remained in the paddocks, near where they could still see and hear their mothers. The others had also wandered off to their pasture, sniffing and sensing about this new terrain. Curious to explore yet tentative in their first few steps away from the umbrella of safety, they were slow to move about. Everything new, yet an air of familiarity and knowing overtaking them with every step. The further away they were from their mothers, the closer they became to each other. They began to travel like a school of fish. Wandering here, check out this. Then wandering over there and checking out that.

One foal began to admonish another - putting him in his place. This young dark bay foal was communicating that his pasture mate needed to stay behind him - he was going to go first and check this thing out. He turned his backend and lined up to lift his back leg and kick out at him. As the back leg began to lift, the other foal moved away and quickly found a place behind. Waiting for permission to move forward and approach the scary thing that was being examined.

We went closer to see who it was that had quickly managed to gain the respect of the weanling herd and assume the role of leader. I was surprised to see it was Dyna's foal. He turned around and I caught a glimpse of the stunning white blaze on his fuzzy dark gangly body. He had her markings, a flashy white blaze, and a single white stocking, like shiny chrome on a vintage car.

My heart warmed and my eyes filled as I witnessed this moment of his rebirth. My daughter and I began wandering back to the mare's paddock, waiting for my son to finish up his chores before walking back up to the house to get ready for school.

We went in to be with Dyna. With tender emotion and a sense of pride pulsing through me, I put my daughter down to go seek out long strands of grass to offer Dyna. I touched Dyna's cheek with my palm. I ran my hand down towards her muzzle, feeling the soft yet prickly touch of her face on my hand. She raised her head up towards my head, then rested her heavy head on my shoulder, and let out a long audible sigh. We stood together in this stillness for what felt like an eternity. Neither of us keen to move first, breaking the unspoken bond we were resting in. My little girl wandered back into the paddock, a handful of long grass in tow, she climbed through the fence rails and stretched out her tiny hand, holding it up to Dyna, a grieving mother, like a sacred offering. Dyna stretched her head down, sniffed the top of my daughter's head, and then took the grass from her outstretched hand. Then she turned around, wandered over to the automatic waterer, and drank for a long time. I wondered how long it had been since she paused from the suffering of separation to replenish herself.

Then Dyna turned and walked out of the paddock and towards the other mares, out grazing in the fields. One mare saw her approaching and ran up to her, inquiring. The two mares sniffed and squealed, alerting the other horses to attention. Dyna and the other mare now trotted towards the larger herd, picking up pace as they approached. Soon they were galloping forward. As they picked up speed, other horses began to run over and join them. Soon the whole band of mares, close to 30 of them, were galloping about, running this way and that, bucking, farting, zigging, and zagging until the energy began to settle and they got back to grazing.

I looked down at my baby girl, eyes wide and brimming with excitement at this display. Always captivated by such animated demonstrations of grace, power, beauty, and movement. She looked up at me and said, *"Dyna not sad anymore momma - look, she happy!!"*

As she spoke, I smiled, squeezed her little body, and then looked out to see Dyna looking towards us. Head held high, body alert, she let out this sharp powerfully emphatic exhale. It felt more like a statement, an exclamation of sorts than an actual exhale.

I felt the air of longing begin to dissipate. I knew that soon; I too would have to leave before I was ready and strike out on my own. I was going to separate from what I'd known, what had become pseudo safe and certain for a life that no longer required me to abandon and reject myself daily.

I was going to have to leave this beautiful place, leave my toxic yet familiar marriage and navigate an unknown path of stress, fear, and anxiety, in order to find my way back to myself. Like Dyna did. Like her baby did.

I wept the whole way back to the house. My daughter inquired why my eyes were leaking and how come I wasn't happy for Dyna like she was. My son now following behind, shielded from his mothers' pain and fear. I hid from them what Dyna hid from no one.

This would be a lesson the horses would offer me again and again. Brutiful transparency. Beautiful + Brutal. The practice of no longer hiding what pained me but honoring it by setting it free.

I was holding them, my babies. And the horses were holding me.

Birth, life, death, re-birth.

Horse as healer

So here is the essential *magic* of horse-human relationships; they help you use emotion as information. By doing so you get to act while in the moment, engage with surprisingly agile responses to environmental stimuli and relationship challenges.

Linda Kohanov in her pioneering books on the intelligence of horse-human bonding, helps us understand that what horses really do when we partner with them in a therapeutic context is this:

(a) Feel the emotion in its purest form
(b) Get the message behind the emotion
(c) Change something in response to the message
(d) Go back to grazing

In other words, let the emotion go, and either get back on task or relax, so you can enjoy life fully. Horses don't hang on to stories, ruminating over the details of uncomfortable situations. They opt for healing over holding on.

Horses have transformed from beasts of burden to cherished allies in the growth and transformation of the human spirit. They have evolved from workhorses, pulling carts, carrying men into battle, and as our main means of transportation to therapeutic allies and beloved partners both in the show ring and in life.

According to the Humane Society of the United States, which reports and tracks the demographics of the equine population, as of 2007, there are over five million horses categorized in the pleasure and recreation category, while there are three million categorized in the breeding, work and competition category. This is a drastically lower number than in the early 1920s where there were over 25 million horses in the United States alone. These early equine reports were conducted by the U.S department of agriculture. ("The demographics of the US equine population")

As of 2008 there are over 40 different ways to describe how to work with horses for the growth, development, and healing of humans. Virtually ALL of the acronyms used include one of these four terms: *assisted, guided, experiential or facilitated. (Strozzi Mazzucchi, 2015, #17)*

Why is this you may wonder? They ***assist*** you to discover what that knot, that lives deep inside your gut is really connected to. They ***guide*** you towards feeling into those gut sensations. They offer you the ***experience*** of feeling supported and held while exploring such sensations. As prey animals, their very way of being in the world *facilitates* a deeply curious noticing. This opportunity to be slightly horse-like in your sensing, noticing, attuning, and responding, based on your own unique inquiry IS the magic of horses.

In its purest form this work we engage in with horses - *equine guided education*, integrates equine interactions, with a kinesthetic experience, along with cognitive reflections to amplify the self-development process.

As I shared in my long-ago experience with Dyna the broodmare and her foal, horses can sense that which lies just beneath, creating an unspoken bond and sense of connection. This connection often creates a willingness to *hear, see and feel* that which previously couldn't be *heard, seen, or felt.*

When I consider over the years, how many people who genuinely cared about me, told me I needed to leave my marriage - I couldn't hear them. When I began to witness how my children's behavior and attachment styles were being directly affected in a negative way - I still couldn't see clearly enough to make a move. I began to lose sleep, develop digestive issues, binge drink in order to numb. I was stuck using my limited coping strategies to avoid feeling what needed to be felt. It wasn't until I woke from a slumber of denial, grief, and wanting to avoid my pain, that I could accept my reality, and begin to change it.

Matters of the Heart

All too often we rely on our minds to solve our problems. As Albert Einstein reminds us *"We cannot solve our problems with the same thinking we used when we created them."*

When we partner with horses we consciously or unconsciously shift from primarily our thinking selves to a more embodied feeling self. As I've preached, it's our thoughts that affect our feelings, which in turn influences our behaviors.

When you enter into a relationship with a horse, you're encouraged to feel first. To connect with the coherence of YOUR unique heart and attend to it while still remaining attuned to the outside world. From this space, insights arise. Shifts occur. Awareness amplifies. Healing begins to happen. A transformation is underway.

Healing isn't something you need to search for. You simply need to seek out and remove the barriers that block healing from naturally occurring. It's like love, and this quote from the beloved Sufi poet Rumi *"Your task is not to seek for love, but merely to seek and find all the barriers within yourself that you have built against it."*

By connecting to and embracing your own heart, you will be able to discover the barriers you've built around it. We all have barriers and wounds of sorts. When you remove these barriers and become willing to expose wounds, healing and love happen naturally.

The way in which we effectively create meaningful connections with horses and each other is through a process of Mind, Body, and Heart. By first gaining the attention of your horse, you have focus, engagement and a thoughtful connection. Next, you invite a connection with their body. Through touch, energy, and intention, we gain the ability to move our horses' body or move with our horse's body. Last, we invite a connection to their heart or the soul. This takes time, trust, and mutual safety. The result is a horse who willingly wants to be with you, who will seek to engage and respond to the coherence of your heart and your heart's desires (Best, C. 2021)

The heart math institute is an organization committed to providing solutions for activating the heart of humanity. The Heart Math Institute empowers individuals, families, groups, and organizations to enhance their life experiences using tools that enable them to better recognize and access their intuitive insight and heart intelligence.

"Recent studies conducted by the Institute of Heart Math provide a clue to explain the bidirectional 'healing' that happens when we are near horses. According to researchers, the heart has a larger electromagnetic field and higher level of intelligence than the brain: A magnetometer can measure the heart's energy field radiating up to 8 to 10 feet around the human body. While this is certainly significant it is perhaps more impressive that the electromagnetic field projected by the horse's heart is five times larger than the human one (imagine a sphere-shaped field that completely surrounds you). The horse's electromagnetic field is also stronger than ours and can actually directly influence our own heart rhythm!

Horses are also likely to have what science has identified as a "coherent" heart rhythm (heart rate pattern) which explains why we may "feel better" when we are around them... studies have found that a coherent heart pattern or HRV is a robust measure of well-being and consistent with emotional states of calm and joy – that is, we exhibit such patterns when we feel positive emotions.

A coherent heart pattern is indicative of a system that can recover and adjust to stressful situations very efficiently. Oftentimes, we only need to be in a horse's presence to feel a sense of wellness and peace. In fact, research shows that people experience many physiological benefits while interacting with horses, including lowered blood pressure and heart rate, increased levels of beta-endorphins (neurotransmitters that serve as pain suppressors), decreased stress levels, reduced feelings of anger, hostility, tension, and anxiety, improved social functioning; and increased feelings of empowerment, trust, patience, and self-efficacy." (Heartmath.org)

Horse Wisdom

One of the purest forms of mirroring in the world of horses is when two horses massage each other. There is something quite tender and highly attuned to their reciprocal way of touching and informing.

Summer and Ginger, two pseudo sister horses you'll meet in the upcoming chapters are captivating in their massaging of each other. This reciprocal touch will often begin with one of the horses siding up to the other and begin to rub the mane or top of the neck, with her muzzle. Summer will start, Ginger will reciprocate. They will simultaneously work their way down the top line of each other's bodies, guiding each other's touch by focusing on an area, motion, and depth of pressure. As one moves, so does the other. The pace, vigor, and aptitude at which their determined muzzles work on each other is a sight to witness.

Mirroring can either be a conscious or unconscious reflection of actions, gestures, communication, or energy. It occurs in the human world, just as it occurs in the horse or natural world.

Horses can sense your (and each other's) heart rate, muscle tension, and depth of breath from about 30 feet away. In nature, a predator who makes a mistake misses a meal. In the wild, if a horse makes a mistake, he faces injury, harm to self or herd mates, or worst-case scenario he's dinner for a predator. These highly instinctive responses haven't left the species, despite the fact that very few of them rarely face this kind of mortal danger in their domesticated lives. Living in barns has kept horses safe and protected, yet their essence is very much still wild and free.

In addition, horses have 340-degree vision, 140-degree range with their ears, and can sense any kind of change in their surroundings *through* each other. Equine expert, author, and researcher Linda Kohanov coins this *socio-sensual awareness.* The human equivalent of socio-sensual awareness is when you *"feel"* the change occur in a room when someone gets angry or upset. Or when someone is grieving, experiencing a sense of deep sadness, there's a particular *'felt sense'* experienced by those present.

Socio-sensual awareness is what makes horses such brilliant partners in the healing, growth, and personal development of humans. They generously mirror for you what's frequently unconscious. A horse can provide almost instant feedback to you about the state of your inner world, whether you're aware of it or not.

They can determine whether you're engaged or blocked in your head, heart or body, simply through interacting with them. In turn, they provide highly attuned, completely authentic feedback to you as you begin to shift.

Want to change the way your mind is always racing from one thought to another? Spend time in a round pen connecting with a horse. Overwhelmed by feelings, driven by your emotions? Try taking a horse for a walk, while tuning into your breath and your step. An intensely physical person, drawn to touch, contact and movement? Practice using minimum essential pressure when grooming a horse. What is it like to actually feel more with less pressure?

As prey animals, horses exist in a nearly constant state of fight, flight, freeze. They have a great deal to teach us how to regulate ourselves naturally. They are masters at conserving their energy and instinctively knowing when to take action.

As horses are present and in the moment at all times, unfamiliar with ruminating about the past or contemplating about the future, their rest and digest, recovery processes are highly contagious to our human experience.

Developing the capacity to just BE with a horse, provides an instantaneous reset for the nervous system. There's nothing quite like taking a few long, slow breaths while standing next to a 1200lb prey animal to deeply ground you and naturally regulate your adrenaline and cortisol levels.

The yin of horse leadership

As horses are no longer required to work in fields and carry us off to war - they are now able to do something much more important. Help us, work on us. Horses relate to the world, primarily from a *'yin'* or feminine perspective. They are successful and effective in their harnessing of feminine values. This looks like cooperation over competition, responsiveness over strategy, emotion and intuition over logic, process over goals, and an overarching creative approach to life, that these qualities engender. (Kohanov, L. 2007, #xxxiii)

Horses respond best to 'true intent' or states of congruency. When your conscious, preoccupied mind becomes calm and responsive, the right solution, answer, or next step becomes known. Call it intuition, spiritual enlightenment, divine intervention, universal guidance, horse wisdom, or some combination of all these attributes. Regardless, realizations acquired through states of congruence seem to be much more innovative, effective, and longer-lasting than those conjured up from a conditioned mind.

Ancient Taoists recommend '*Know the yang, but keep to the yin*' otherwise stated, know the masculine but keep to the feminine. When a patriarchal culture such as ours keeps to the yang, we remain conquest oriented, we discount and degrade the feminine, we lose our ability to harmonize with each other and our natural world. (Kohanov, L. 2007 #86)

Ultimately, what we seek here is a balance between energies. A dynamic interplay between an empathetic and considerate form of masculine energy intertwined with a heightened sense of feminine power and an increased sense of agency.

By understanding leadership styles when partnering with horses, you gain clarity and vision to become the kind of mother, partner, sister, friend, and leader that you desire. By modeling a more thoughtful and compassionate approach, what you're really doing is engaging in '*passive leadership*'. This implies a strong, steady, confident, yet relaxed energetic quality. One where you don't cause undue stress and anxiety to your people, and where you're mindful to conserve your energy for when you really need it.

When humans become more horse-like, we all win.

Practice

Journal reflection questions

- Consider your relationship with the birth - life- death- rebirth cycle? What experiences have you had where you witnessed this play out? What was it like for you?

- What's your relationship like with your heart, the desires of your heart, and your ability to connect with the essence of your own heart's frequency?

- Reflect on your current leadership style. How do you summarize the way you lead your life, your family, your home, your workplace? Is it more masculine or feminine in nature? How is it working for you?

- What does the concept of true intent or fundamental will bring up within you? Do you have a sense of what this feels like or looks like in your life?

CHAPTER 5 – NATURES WAYS

"In learning to call on the medicine of any person, creature or natural force, one must maintain an attitude of reverence and be willing to accept assistance." – J. Sams and D. Carson (Medicine Cards)

Mother Earth and Father Time

How very special are we
For just a moment to be
Part of life's eternal rhyme
How very special are we
To have on our family tree
Mother Earth and Father Time

He turns the seasons around
And so, she changes her gown
But they always look in their prime
They go on dancing their dance
Of every lasting romance
Mother Earth and Father Time

The summer larks return to sing
Oh, what a gift they give
Then autumn days grow short and cold
Oh, what a joy to live

How very special are we
For just a moment to be
Part of life's eternal rhyme
How very special are we
To have on our family tree
Mother Earth and Father Time

Do you remember listening to this song as a child in the movie *Charlotte's Web*? Even then, as an eight-year-old girl, I recall being blown away by the wisdom and generosity of this spider momma. How did she know so much, being a tiny spider? That voice of hers, so mesmerizing and comforting despite such uncertainty. How could she know she was going to die, leave her spider babies all alone and be totally ok with that? Eight-year-old mind blown.

When I watched this again as an adult with my own kids, I recall them asking some of the same questions. "Why would a pig's best friend be a spider, it doesn't make sense, they can't even play together, dumb!" My seven-year-old son denounced. We were living on our family's 300-acre working horse ranch in the heart of BC's Cariboo at the time. We had over 100 horses, a few goats, an assortment of cattle, a dozen or so chickens, and a handful of cats and dogs. We had both witnessed uniquely interesting relationships between various animal species by this time.

I reminded my son about that quirky chicken we had who was never more than a few feet away from one of the horses. This fluffy white bird would lay her eggs in the hay feeder, where this particular horse would graze. She'd perch herself on the fence as close as possible to where the horses gathered.

Wherever Silver the horse would wander in the paddock, this little hen would follow. When Silver would lie down, tucking his long legs near to his body, the chicken would either cuddle up near his belly or perch on top of his back and rest there. They moved together with a sense of ease and care that we'd not witnessed before in such a cross-species bond.

I wonder now about the uncommon communication that occurred between them. The comfort they may have provided to each other. The wisdom, safety, kinship, and alliance they cultivated and why?

The horse and the hen. A not so regular farmyard fairy tale.

The bonds between animal species are as mysterious as the bonds between humans and animals.

There is something there beyond words, that often transcends our limited understanding.

This reminds me of the Netflix Series 'My Octopus Teacher'. If you haven't seen it yet, it's a must-watch. The story beautifully and artistically captures a bond between the intelligence of the octopus and the sensitivities of the man. Theirs is a story that transcends all understanding, all reason. Without interfering or disrupting the natural rhythm, this man bears witness to the nuanced lifecycle of the octopus and becomes a part of it. He crosses a threshold and becomes deeply involved, invested in playing a role in Mother Nature's great story.

Nature has her ways. The mysterious relationship between Mother Earth and Father time reminds us that we are all a part of a much larger, more intricate plan. That our limited time here matters. What we do with it and how we show up matters, we are all a part of this particular family tree. This web of life. An interplay between time and space.

In my experience, Nature heals but Time does not. Contrary to the proverb *'time heals all wounds'* from Greek poet Menander, who lived around 300 B.C. Time does not heal all wounds. It can often feel like a slap in the face to hear such words amidst deep grief, or complex trauma. Trauma research reveals that if you ignore that which pains you, these wounds get bigger and lead to negative fallout in other areas. If you attend to it, learn about it, give it your attention, intention and support over time, THAT is what will help inspire healing. Not time alone.

Time + Compassion + Action = Healing.

Animal Medicine

The concept of 'medicine' originates from our First Nations, Indigenous, and Native American peoples. The medicine they refer to is anything that improves one's connection to the Great Mystery and to all of life (Sams, Carson, 1999, #14).

Consider experiences you've had with certain animals that have spoken to you or touched you somehow. Is there a particular species that whispers to you, that occupies your dreams? Maybe you're captivated by bald eagles, have an affinity for dolphins, a kinship with wolves, an alliance to the spirit of bears, or synchronicity with dragonflies? When energetic exchanges like this occur, it's often an insight into the ways of power. Your nature-based power ally is a certain animal with which you recognize an important connection. This kind of power is one that comes from the idea of unity. Of each being, having within itself some aspect of all other beings. It is the law of oneness. (Sams, Carson, 1999, #14)

The need for guidance from animals, of being in the presence of their unique medicine is a type of guidance in high demand today. As we exist in a time that has severed itself from nature, in all her magical and mysterious ways, communing with animal energy is a remedy for this dissociation. It is a healing for those of us who've become overly attached to civilization and caught up in the process of becoming *'denatured'*.

As the wisdom of this book is focused on the medicine of horses, and you are the one reading, there may be something about the inherent nature of horses that speaks to you. Quite possibly you're a rider or horsewoman yourself, keen to learn and absorb from other horsewoman. Legendary horsewoman Lee McLean's words linger in my mind often when considering my evolving riding relationship with horses. She suggests that a gentler, wiser approach to riding over one's lifetime would be to *'practice being a little bit better, most of the time.'* It's unrealistic and also unkind to ask your horse to be better than you are. Therefore, a continued commitment to opt for a little bit better most of the time feels much more aligned than the frequently used quote in the horse world; *'practice doesn't make perfect, 'perfect practice makes perfect.'*

If you're not a rider or drawn to horses in a relationship that involves a partnership of movement, then maybe it's their power or agility that intrigues you. The way they move so magnificently with such apparent ease and grace. Maybe it's their timid curiosity and thoughtful noticing. Or is their sense of freedom and wildness that inspires something within you. Quite possibly it's the way they smell, the touch of your hand on their coat, or the feel of their whiskers and muzzle on your palm. Or maybe it's the surprising sense of calm and quiet you feel within when you're near them. How time slows and you're transported into what feels like another dimension. Only here and now, remain. No past. No future. Just this moment in their presence. Possibly, it's all of the above. Whatever *'it'* is, you are not alone in being captivated by the magnificence of horse medicine.

As we explore the topic of Horse Medicine, let me introduce you to five of the horses who've played significant roles in the healing journey of hundreds of clients over this last decade.

Ginger & Summer

Meet Ginger and Summer. I introduce them together, as that is how they roll. Always together.

Ginger is a 12-year-old Cob, her coat is delicious shades of dark brown, she has white stockings up to her knees and a big beautiful white blaze that runs down her face. Her shaggy forelock hangs down over her eyes giving a wildish bohemian - gypsy-like quality to her. Ginger is the *heart horse*. She has an inner radar that instantly picks up on matters of the heart. A broken heart, blocks in the heart chakra, inability to give or receive love freely, worthiness around love, fear of love, loss of love… Whatever frequency is vibrating highest, if it resides in the heart, Ginger will show up. She will be the first to approach, she will come near or right up to. She will often make contact with her head, with either the front of the chest/heart area or the back, sometimes both. She will hold precious space for the healing of the heart to occur. Sometimes she will absorb the energy of the human in her presence and then model what it looks like to actively release discomfort, pain, and anxiety then get back to grazing. Hers is a gentle, loving, kind-hearted sentience who's medicine is a gentle blessing to many.

Summer: Summer is Ginger's BFF, her soul sister - where one goes the other is sure to follow. They are two of a kind. Summer is a 20-year-old quarter horse mare; she was raised at the ranch in the Cariboo as a roping and barrel racing horse. She is living her best life now. Semi-retired, respected within her herd, an elder with potent medicine to share. Summer is the *feelings horse.* She's the first to approach, express curiosity, or capture attention if there are unresolved or conflictual feelings present. If there are difficult emotions to process, or if there are emotions being avoided or repressed, she will sense it. Hers is a quiet, tender, soft energy. She will often stand very close and very still and invite feelings to arise.

People often cry in her presence without knowing exactly why or where it comes from. Often, she'll begin to move her body, twitch, shake and become animated with her ears, as emotions begin to move through the individual. She invites a leaning in towards feelings. Often individuals will find themselves leaning their whole bodies against her, wrapping their arms around in a horse-hug, or leaning backward against her barrel and back. Her soft strength and tender spirit offer a sense of safety as individuals explore their own emotional congruence.

Aloe

Aloe: Aloe possesses the lone wolf archetype. Confidently aloof, indifferent, and somewhat adolescent in her energy. She's a 10-year-old thoroughbred, draft horse cross. She has the energy of a draft horse and the power of a thoroughbred. She's what I consider the *transitions horse*. As she herself has recently integrated her own dharma around life transitions, she's become quite astute at holding space for others to do the same.

She will often be the horse individuals are drawn to when they are in fear, or navigating fear, stress, and anxiety. She demonstrates a steadiness and inner confidence that is not acutely affected by the vibration of an individuals' angst, insecurity, or fear. She is a safe haven, a beacon of solidarity as people work through their fears and begin to harness their own inner strength and resiliency. Aloe is also uber lazy. She's a master at conserving her energy. She calls those interacting with her to become connected to their true intent. If you were to ask her to go or move her body, yet deep down unsure or not fully committed to the ask, she'll know it and she will not move for you. She offers you opportunities to commit to yourself, to know what it is you want, and to learn how to ask for it. She is generous and forgiving, patient and kind-hearted. She can be silly and lighthearted, reminding us to not take ourselves so seriously. With Aloe, you learn to laugh, smile, lighten up and kick up your heels. She will often model discharging anxiety and emotion in a myriad of ways, reminding you to opt for healing over holding on.

Biscuit

Meet Biscuit, a sweet treat. This *16-year-old* quarter horse mare was born at the Cariboo ranch and has what's considered impeccable breeding. Meaning, her parents and their parents all possess the traits, skills, and natural abilities to excel in the disciplines of reining and cow horse work. Biscuit is a sweet treat, a cookie pie. She is candy in horse form. She exudes warmth and willingness, kindness and gentility. She's a "yes" horse.

Whatever you want to do or try, wherever you want to go, and however fast you want to go there, she's in. She's like the friend you can count on who is always ready to go at a moment's notice. Biscuit comes from a lineage of potent mares. Her mother and grandmother were impressive horses, long-lived and impactful in their lives. They accomplished a great deal, but more than that they were deeply cherished by those who owned them until their dying day. Biscuit is pure gold at addressing those who approach her. She graciously attempts while honoring limitations. She creates attachments and then navigates her attachments in a way that inspires compassion and empathy, not only for her but for oneself also. She is masterful at gently and lovingly reflecting the conflicts that can occur within the inner world and outer world of an individual. She is the essence of compassion and kindness.

Gwen

Meet Gwen: I often consider Gwen as the *boundaries* horse. She has an essence of *the trickster* archetype. This big, goofy, awkward horse is a seven-year-old Canadian Warmblood. She is a beautiful mover, jumps fences, and glides gracefully under saddle. She's ticklish, and quirky and often looks like a big giraffe as she meanders around the arena. Gwen will bite you. I can't say for certain why or when, but she will. Gwen will invite you to honor your boundaries and demand you honor hers. She will communicate clearly and then act to enforce. She is masterful at putting up boundaries and offers endless opportunities to practice being in a relationship with her, boundaries in tack. Her jovial, juvenile energy keeps you on your toes while inviting you to not always take yourself too seriously. She's curious but impatient, willing but easily irritated. Gwen decides how she wants to interact and with whom. She will initiate and then end it. She offers an understanding of the complexity of relationships, and insight into the forever changing landscape of desire in action. She will give you the permission you may need to practice putting up fiercely self-loving boundaries.

Tony

Meet Tony: This is Tony, and his owner Sarah. Tony is the lead male horse. He is a stunning 16'3 hand thoroughbred, draft cross. He is a dark dark brown with a closely cropped mane and he is as strong, determined, and powerful as a horse gets. Tony is a full sister to Bagheera. Although they differ in appearance, they share a common connection. They are both confident and powerful in their own right. Tony is the epitome of the *war horse archetype.* He carries his riders into the competition ring, over jumps and cross-country courses, through obstacles, and over them. He carries kids, and seniors, young women, and old men. He is not discerning on his task, he shows up and does his best, every single time. He is who you want by your side when a battle is near. He is fierce and firm, stoic and steadfast. He intimidates most and captivates all. He is a tall, handsome, majestic beauty. The epitome of the strong, silent male. Suffering in silence, dutiful and integrous. He rarely volunteers himself, but instead is chosen. He is less drawn to an individual than they are to him. If there's a battle within, or an erroneous challenge to overcome, the medicine of Tony is where you will land. His innate boldness, courage, and fortitude is a healing balm to energetically absorb. His grace and elegance capture the heart, while his determination and power activate the spirit. He puts individuals in touch with any fear they may have of their own power. For women, the energy of Tony may be a nudge towards harnessing the masculine. A need to at times, get ready to get shit done. You might not like it; it isn't always easy - his energy is a reminder of the strength we all possess that enables us to rise above and tackle the challenge head-on.

Seasons over Balance

For everything, there is a season,
A time for every activity under heaven.
A time to be born and a time to die.
A time to plant and a time to harvest.
A time to kill and a time to heal.
A time to tear down and a time to build up.
A time to cry and a time to laugh.
A time to grieve and a time to dance.
A time to scatter stones and a time to gather stones.
A time to embrace and a time to turn away.
A time to search and a time to quit searching.
A time to keep and a time to throw away.
A time to tear and a time to mend.
A time to be quiet and a time to speak.
A time to love and a time to hate.
A time for war and a time for peace. (the bible, n.d., #)

As much as early experiences with church culture and fundamentalist Christian ideals can be damaging and toxic to women's development, there are many gems of wisdom within the pages of the bible. This verse is one of them.

We love the idea of balance. We are people, who are always seeking SOME sort of balance. Be it on the ground or on horseback, balance is a thing.

A Balance between work and home.
A Balance between firm and kind.
A Balance between rest and play.
A Balance between light and dark.
A Balance between strength and flexibility.
A Balance between being open-hearted and having boundaries
A Balance between our masculine and our feminine
A balance between doing and being.
A balance between being too far forward to too far back.

Eesh ... it can be exhausting navigating such balances. Unless you're a master yogi, devoting your life to the pursuit of extreme flexibility and an unflinching evenness, balance is an unachievable state. At Least for very long. Let's also acknowledge that most of the women we know are not just navigating their own balance, but more often than not, they are the ones assuming responsibility for the balance of others. Their home, their families or children, and some aspects of their work environments. That is one hell-uva balancing act to pull off.

I have come to believe that balance is bullshit.

I have come to know that rhythm, flow, and living in sync with the seasons and transitions of life is where we find a much greater sense of peace and harmonious living.

Indeed, there is a time for all things, a season for all things. Not a word is spoken about a balance of all things. Balance is a man-made idea, one that has not served us very well to date.

Deciding to embrace rhythm and alignment over balance looks like a truthful honoring of the season that you are in.

Wisdom from the First Nation peoples by way of the Medicine Wheel reminds us that it is wise to consider balance in regard to these four categories: Body - Mind - Emotions - Spirit.

Living in balance, therefore suggests incorporating these four aspects of our SELF while navigating the rhythm and flow of the season we find ourselves in.

As a mother of young children and a growing business, it's likely a struggle in daily rhythm to return to school to obtain your master's or Ph.D. at this time.

As you're eagerly nurturing a new romantic relationship, it's likely out of relational alignment to take a work contract that has you traveling 3 weeks out of 4.

As you actively address some recurring health issues, it's likely out of harmony with your body to also sign up for a triathlon.

As you invest in starting your new business, it's likely out of sync to also plan a backpacking trip around South America.

As you learn to find stability in the saddle at a trot, it's not yet time to join a group lesson where they are cantering over poles.

Any one of these crossroads is viable, plausible, and even necessary at times.

I believe women can find a way to manage almost anything. We have already for centuries. We can't however do everything at the same time. Certainly not well.

It is a very real challenge to focus consistently on growing a business while travelling by backpack to remote areas.

It's mighty difficult to mentally focus on academic learning while still navigating sleepless nights with small children. It's physically destabilizing and potentially damaging to train for a triathlon while healing an auto-immune condition.

It's potentially unsafe to canter over poles with three other horse-human pairs in an arena when you're still learning how to create stability for yourself at trot.

You get where I'm going here…. there is a rhythm to life. There is a season for all of it.

To find balance then means to attend to your whole self while navigating the flow of your current reality.

There are general aspects or areas of life that take up our time, make up our days and bring us satisfaction and purpose.

Here is a quick synopsis of focus areas, consider any others you'd add to this list:

Mental/Emotional/Physical Health - your overall wellness

- Parenting, raising healthy kids

- Growing your career, advancing your work

- Building, buying, renovating, developing your home or property

- Healing or nurturing extended family relationships

- Building community connections (clubs, organizations, committees, projects)

- Creativity and Play - what lights you up, remember the fun stuff?

- Growing your social network/connection building (building or deepening friendships)

- Faith, religion, and spirituality - nurturing your spirit and soul

- Healing trauma, overcoming adversity (therapy, various healing modalities)

Full disclosure: I'm guilty of trying to juggle ALL of these varied aspects or *seasons* in life at the same time.

Yes, mam. I too drank the *'you can do it all and have it all'* bewildered tasting feminist Kool-Aid during my early adulthood. It was a noble place to hide out. Avoiding the painfully difficult decisions I knew beckoned, by throwing myself into everything on that list above. I was going to DO it all.

I, after all, was a human DO-ing.

I tried desperately to navigate my failing marriage, be a cool mom, grow my small business, care for our horses all while developing and restructuring our land. I played soccer, hit the gym, took my kids to their soccer games, and traveled for their elite hockey. I was in therapy, both couples and on my own. I was working on the complex relationship with my mother, I was attending church and midweek study groups. I was on two committees and volunteered at my daughters' school.

I was floundering. Lost to myself. Moving all the time. Feeling very little. Thinking, analyzing, criticizing.

I wasn't able to maintain any kind of real or sustainable balance. Overwhelmed, under-inspired, and operating on an unconscious autopilot, I was repeating patterns of behavior I loathed and felt an enormous sense of shame, and guilt around all of it. I felt like an imposter in my own life. Waiting for the other shoe to drop or a better version of 'me' to miraculously arrive, saving myself from myself.

I was drinking too often, dabbling in self-administered anxiety meds, and in a wrestling match with both fear and control. Living with a diminished sense of my own worth and value, and way out of alignment, I felt terrified that my children, witnessing this 'way of life' would come to believe it was fine and good, healthy and normal.

They'd either accept the way of living I was modeling for them and perpetuate it themselves or at some point, they'd come to realize it was dysfunctional, reject how I was choosing to live, and in turn reject me.

This fear ate me up. You know that kind of fear that keeps you up at night. You fall asleep fretting about it and wake up with a clenched jaw, hoping half a pot of coffee will cure the soul level fatigue.

I had energetically invested in all ten of those areas above, all at the same time, full steam ahead. I believed the stories; I was sold on the idea that I could balance it all. If I could just find more time, get more help, make more money, get up earlier, try harder, strive a bit further…. Then it would all fall into place. Joy and peace were experiences that awaited me in the future when I finally got that something, I didn't think I had and desperately needed.

I'm certain you're familiar with this sort of internal battle. The seeking outside yourself - the whispers that feed the longings. Always desiring never satisfying. When you find it, get it, have it, then you'll feel better, enough, sane, whole…at peace with what it.

A woman's best friend, as she navigates the shift from balanced living to seasonal living, living for self instead of living for others is **boundaries**.

Boundaries is the space needed in order to love yourself and another at the same time. Useful boundaries are flexible in nature. They may shift and change as relationships shift and change. They are neither rigid, nor are they weak.

In order to honour your boundaries, what do you need to say NO to? What no longer feels inspiring, aligned, and easy to take action on?

By starting there, you're honoring your own capacity while opening to greater joy and peace now.

Balance is a manmade agenda. One that results in women living overwhelming, restless, and unsatisfying lives. Living in sync with the seasons honors the temporal season you're in, and keeps you connected to the wisdom of life's natural cycles. The ebbs and the flows. The dance between times of doing and times of being.

"The psyches and souls of women also have their own cycles and seasons of doing and solitude, running and staying, being involved and being removed, questing and resting, creating and incubating, being of the world and returning to the soul-place." (Pinoka Estes, 1992. #125

Wisdom of the body

Our bodies know. Our body holds all of our history, our experiences, and our memories. Yes, you can tell your mind to think different thoughts and begin generating new thought patterns, but we also need to connect those thoughts to our body's felt experience and to our spiritual foundation.

"Most psychologists treat the mind as disembodied, a phenomenon with little to no connection to the physical body. Conversely, physicians treat the body with no regard to the mind or the emotions. But the body and mind are not separate, and we cannot treat one without the other." Offers Dr. Candace Pert, known as the goddess of neuroscience.

This is the work of attuning to our somatic self. The word *somatic is* Greek, and it generally translates as *"the living body in its wholeness: the mind, the body, and the spirit as a unity."* When working alongside horses, we use somatics as a guide for facilitating an inquiry. Your unique historical and conditioned responses to your earlier experiences are considered. Your mental decipher-ing, or cognitive interpretations are also woven into the web of understanding. Then through repeat behavior you create change through intentional thought and action. (Strozzi Mazzucchi, # 135)

Anne's Walk with Horses

Anne caught a ferry and rode in her car over three hours to come for a session with the horses. Encouraged by a fellow health and wellness practi-tioner to access support in exploring the stress, anxiety and restlessness that had been rising to the surface, Anne reached out to me.

As Anne began her introduction to the horses, she was immediately aware of her shifting bodily sensations. As we walked into the horse paddock together, Anne became increasingly shifty, restless, twitchy even, displaying a level of discomfort. We paused here and began our inquiry.

"Anne, I'm curious what you're noticing right now?" I asked her.

Anne paused; tears began to well up at the corner of her eyes. She looked to the horses, all five of them had their backs to her and were happily grazing away at their feed stations.

"I feel exactly like I do in most social situations. Like I'm on the outside looking in. I used to go to parties or social gatherings, and I wouldn't know who to approach or how to approach them. So, I'd head over to the bar, get lubricated and then I wouldn't care so much about meeting and greeting. I'd be slightly drunk, sometimes completely drunk, act like a disgracious fool and then deal with the emotionally loaded hangover the days after.... I had so much self-loathing, and no idea how to address it."

As Anne shared about her past experience and how it was revisiting her in this present moment experience with the horses, the mare Summer looked up at her, met her gaze, held it for a time and then returned back to grazing. Exhaling before she resumed pulling hay through a large hanging hay net.

"What did that look from that horse feel like to you just then Anne?" I inquire. Anne pauses, and continues to stare in the direction of Summer.

"It felt like an acknowledgement." Anne's eyes dried. She held her gaze on Summer and became still and, somewhat taller, more solid within herself.

"It felt like she saw me just then and acknowledged me. She didn't look over me or through me, she looked right at me, saw me and didn't move away, but stayed put." Anne's eyes began to tear up.

"Oh my god, I don't know why I'm crying right now. Wow, this feels very deep. I wasn't expecting this." Anne half laughs before carrying on. *"What else did you notice in that interaction between you and Summer?"* I nudge her further, seeing if there's anything else that will emerge when given space, room and permission.

Anne pauses for a moment, tipping her head to one side, then the other, then she replies, *"after she looked at me with that look, she had that long exhale, and then went back to eating, why did she do that. Does that mean something?"*

I reply to Anne *"Horses only do things because there is a reason. There is almost always a meaning behind their behaviour and the timing for it. Horses are masters at conserving their energy, unlike us, if they act there is purpose. Do you think there was a message for you connected to that exhale at that particular moment?"*

Anne again pauses to hear my question and takes it in. She looks at Summer, then back at me before responding. Before she replies, again Summer looks at Anne and lets out another powerful exhale, then returns to grazing.

Anne attempts to bring words to her wonderings, to vocalize that which she senses down deep, bravely she offers up

"Maybe she was exhaling as a way to release something? I think she was telling me through that exhale to let go of the suffering and shame I'm holding onto from that time in my life where I was a train wreck and hurt others and myself. I feel like she was showing me how to let it go, get over myself and just carry on living my life. Geez that sounds so simple when I hear myself say it."

I smile at Anne and move closer to her so we're standing side by side, looking towards Summer who's happily grazing away. The somatics of Anne's body shifted significantly from when she first entered the paddock with the horses. Her shoulders slack, her head cocked to one side, gazing softly at Summer. Her hands still, resting by her side. Standing steady within herself and rooted to the ground.

"Pause here for a moment Anne and scan your body. Start at the top of your head, and just allow your awareness to travel down all sides of your body. Like someone is pouring a big basin of warm water over your head, let your awareness travel like water over yourself. Follow this awareness until it meets at a pool around your feet. What sensations do you notice? Where do you notice them? Do they feel familiar or new? Can you describe what you feel?" I invite Anne to reconnect with the wisdom of her body. To get curious about what she notices from a somatics lens and to practice increasing her ability to access the sensations and name them while remaining curious about what information this may provide her.

"Uh, wow I feel somehow much lighter than I did 15 minuets ago. I've been in therapy off and on for years now and I have never felt that much shift in any of my one-hour sessions let alone in the first fifteen minutes." Anne proclaims, laughing out loud and shaking her head in disbelief. *"I feel space around my lower belly and a sense of calm. Often this part of my body feels tight, and uncomfortable. I also noticed that my head feels clear, less thoughts racing about or a greater sense of calm maybe. There is a heaviness around my heart, something there..."*

Summer steps towards Anne as we discuss what sensations and energy she notices within. I urge Anne to respond as she chooses to Summer's forward advance.

"What should I do?" Anne asks

I suggest she focus on her heart. How can she connect with her heart, with the support of Summer's heart? Summer takes another step forward and pauses. Looking inquisitively at Anne and me.

Anne walks towards Summer, slowly and cautiously. She touches Summers's face and runs her hand down her neck. Summers eyes close somewhat, expressing relaxation and a sense of safety.

Hand on her own heart, Anne looks into Summers sleepy eye and asks, *"How do I connect with her heart?"*

"If you're comfortable, why don't you slowly move your heart towards her heart. Keep the connection you have with your own heart frequency, picture it in your mind's eye and slowly move towards hers. See what happens. She will either stay and lean in, or she may choose to go. She has free will here as do you, to connect from a heart space." I invite Anne to explore the coherence of her heart in the willing presence of Summer.

During the next half hour Summer stands unmoving, as Anne leans the front of her heart into Summers body. Soon she turns around and has draped the back of her heart over Summers's midsection. Breathing together in stillness, there's a sense of nurturing occurring in this exchange.

Soon Anne stands up, wraps her arms around Summer's neck in an embrace and slowly begins to move towards me.

Summer takes a few steps towards her friend Ginger, exhales loudly and shakes her whole body like a dog who's just had a bath. Literally shaking off any residual energy from her exchange with Anne, and then getting back to grazing alongside Ginger.

After we wrap up our session together and Anne prepares to leave, I encourage her to consider this a new foundation to build on. A lived experience of acceptance and heartfelt connections that contradicts her earlier ones. She is free to build whatever she desires atop of this foundation of calm, steadiness and true connection she is architecting within. The more experiences she has that directly contradicts her earlier ones, the more profoundly she will be able to rewire her brain and offer her nervous system opportunities to recover.

"Return to that felt sense of being truly seen and accepted again and again. Come up with a statement or a declaration that feels true for you based on that experience. Write it down, hang it on your mirror, say it to yourself as if it's coming out of Summer's mouth. Absorb it as truth, practice this repatterning as often and in as many varied moments as you can." I say to her as she steps towards her car, a heartfelt kinship for Anne growing.

Anne nods. *"I have my journal with me, I already know I'm going to spend the ferry ride pouring out onto paper."*

This process never ceases to amaze me. What has felt like my mess, has evolved into my medicine. What was my own medicine, is now becoming my mastery. A connection to horses, ranching, and farm life, the inspiration that sparked in childhood has evolved into a practice with therapeutic value for both humans and horses alike.

I have the privilege of witnessing Anne's evolution. Her life is transforming. She is vibrant, alive, and following her creative aspirations. Her life is unfolding in fascinating ways beyond her own understanding. The work she is doing to invite in the healing is transforming her relationships, her work life, and her creative passions. I am honored to witness the evolution of such powerful women in the world.

The wisdom of the body isn't an experience that belongs solely to us humans. Horses experience similar mind-body connections. If one person goes into the paddock with their helmet, riding boots, and gloves on, dangles the halter and walks towards Tony (the Warhorse archetype) with the intention to catch him and get him ready to go for a ride, he will almost always walk away. Sometimes he'll run. After a time, he will soften to the request to be caught or else the rider will give up and likely seek out some form of help. If you walk into the paddock with the wheelbarrow and manure rake, or if you have no halter and approach simply out of curiosity, Tony will almost always stay. He will not leave or walk away, sometimes he will come up and approach you. Meeting your open agenda, your needing or wanting nothing of him at this moment, Tony will relax.

For Tony, relaxing in the presence of people who want or need nothing from him but to observe or connect if he's interested, has therapeutic value for him. Horses are sentient beings after all - able to feel and perceive things. Some more deeply than others. Exchanges with horses where the interaction is solely based on a human-initiated interaction limit the benefits to both horses and humans. The types of exploratory, mindful interactions with horses I'm speaking to here, provide them opportunities to express themselves freely and explore their preferences. When it comes to connection, touch, energy, and engagement, horses have a mind and heart of their own. They're social animals after all. Living in herds and interacting with each other on a daily basis is one of the major contributors to keeping a horse mentally and physically healthy and content throughout its lifetime.

We are all just animals living in nature together. Navigating our ever-changing internal and external environments. We're not that different really. Consider Tony, might he remind you of someone you know? Does his experience in any way shape or form feel relatable?

Animals have an extreme sense of perception. Especially prey animals. Their very survival is based on these perceptions and sensitivities. To varying degrees, we all have extreme perceptions the same way animals do, because we all have animal brains.

If we can begin to home in on how to use the sensory processing parts of our brain the way animals do, we can make conscious and bring meaning to these sensitivities. (Grandin, 2005)

That's why being more 'horse-like' can yield positive results for the body, mind, and spiritual health of a human.

In our sessions together, Anne practiced being more horse-like. She felt into the somatics of her body. She noticed the tension and restlessness arising in her physical self. She inquired within, as to what was underneath those sensations. What feelings, experiences, memories those sensations were connected to. She became still, grounded, and present to what was, she cultivated a sense of willingness to explore more and remain curious.

She was directed towards an opportunity for healing. By remaining connected to her senses, open and curious, supported and held by the collective energy of the moment, Anne experienced some recovery. On a level deeper than the physical layer, Anne's subtle body became activated, energy moved through and out. Anne participated fully in an experience that gave her a sense of calm and connection, mind-body, and heart. She reported a feeling of steadiness and clarity not present prior to her experience with the horses.

Anne's humor, tenderness, and inner beauty are more brilliant every time our paths cross. There's freedom about someone in the midst of telling a new story. When you reauthor your story through the lens of having healed it, what you attract into your life can change dramatically. Gone is that sense of striving and yearning. What is aligned and meant to compliment your highest self begins to show up, with varying degrees of ease and effort.

Practice

Self-reflection Journaling

- Describe the season of life you're in, what feels most important to you at this particular stage of your life?

- What comes up for you as you read about balance and attending to your body-mind-emotions - spirit?

- If boundaries are tricky for you, you're so-so about enforcing them, they waffle or they're weak, inquire why you think that is. Are there feelings present in the body behind the experience of boundaries?

- What might the Somatics of your body be guiding you towards? If you really listened, what might your body tell you?

CHAPTER 6 –
THE REMEDY OF EMBRACING
A HEALING PATH

"As my sufferings mounted, I soon realized that there were
two ways in which I could respond to my situation -- either
to react with bitterness or seek to transform the suffering into
a creative force. I decided to follow the latter course."
—*Martin Luther King Jr.*

The first law of healing may sound simple, but often it can be the most challenging to embody. The first law of healing is to love the things you care about. The essence of healing can be defined as *loving of and caring for.*

This may seem overly simplified, but that's all it takes to begin to heal. The first and foremost task when addressing your healing or growth is to look at any blocks or barriers you have consciously or unconsciously created around loving and caring for yourself. Then notice any blocks or barriers you may have around the loving and caring of others.

Whether it's a fractured or strained relationship or an undesirable aspect of yourself, healing becomes possible when you become crystal clear on what it is you care about and determine how to begin caring for it sufficiently.

Your body, your family, your home, your work…. What's required in order for you to love what you care about right now, just as it is. Not later, when everything may or may not be ideally how you want it, but right now in this present moment. Exactly as you are, warts and all.

To love your shape, your skin, your face your age. To honor these parts of yourself.

To love your people, your relationships, the things you do together, the way you feel about each other.

To love your home, where it is that you live, where you cook your food, rest your head, and commune together. To love your work, what you do to provide support and resources, how you do it, why you do it, and who you do it with.

What you cannot skip over, what MUST come first in this order of healing is this: *Love yourself first*. Let this love and care naturally rise up and out of you from the love, honor, and respect you have cultivated from within you.

There is a place within each of us very near our core, it is our knowing, loving and caring center. It is not affected by thoughts or ideas of who you should be or how others want you to be, but a place within where you belong to yourself, without the need for anything external.

In order to transcend your human limitations and quiet your critical mind, you must practice connecting with this aspect of your essential self. Maybe this aspect of yourself feels nearest when you're in the forest or walking along the beach or lakeshore. Maybe this connection to your essential self feels near when you're playing with children or interacting with beloved pets or horses. Maybe this aspect of yourself hasn't yet been given the permission it needs to make herself visible or felt by you. Wherever you land here, know that the freedom you desire is directly connected to knowing, loving, and accepting your truest self.

To heal is to exhibit genuine care for the things you love.

Don't be confused any longer, we often get it backward. You withhold love and care until the body is thinner, or the face is prettier. You observe your body, your *'self'* like it is a problem to be solved.

You often end up attacking your body, and yourself. You bully and cajole trying and failing to get the love and acceptance you desire. You buy into industry standards of beauty, endlessly trying to keep up with societal trends and seek (either conscious or unconscious) validation of what others think or feel about you.

When you seek acceptance and love, pursue belonging and worthiness from anywhere other than your own true self first, you are breaking the first law of healing. You are going against yourself.

Imagine putting more energy into who you really are, and less into how you act, what you look like and how others view you. The merciless task to remove signs of aging, shrink your waist, enlarge your boobs, lift your butt is an exhausting merry-go-round. One sure to leave you dizzy and distressed. Never really content with the skin you're in.

Did you know that only 4% of women around the entire world consider themselves beautiful, and 92% of teen girls would like to change something about the way they look? 80% of women agree that every woman has something about her that is beautiful but does not see their own beauty. More than half of women globally (54%) agree that when it comes to how they look, they are their own worst beauty critic.

This research came through a study Dove sponsored called *"The real truth about beauty revisited."*

When I look around at the sheer volume of beautiful, stunning women I know from various parts of the world, I am blown away by our own dismissal and rejection of our inherent beauty. It breaks my heart for us. The useless suffering, we inflict upon ourselves. What a damn waste of enjoyment and satisfaction!

There is a moment when you will come back home to yourself and think *"Hells Yes! This is who I am and am grateful to be."* Those moments you know, beyond a shadow of a doubt that you are precious, unique, and wholly worthy just as you are. Regardless of arbitrary external influences. You are not better, nor are you worse, than any other living being. Nope, not perfect, who is!? It's an illusion, a trickery. Women are always the loser of the perfection game. Tap into the knowing that you are enough. Now, just as you are. Hold onto this truth. It will see you through the ups and downs, ebbs and flows, and continue to lead you home. Back to yourself.

Core Desired Feelings

This is where things can get interesting. This is where you get to experience a taste of your inner agency. Your own phenomenal will. Gain clarity on your true intent. Your brilliant and beautiful divine power. It's how you will move beyond entrenched patterns, old traumas, a dysfunctional family upbringing, or chaotic and anxiety-inducing experiences.

Right now, decide how it is you really want to feel in your life. The strategy is simple. Start with the heart. Return to the heart. The heart holds your truth and power resides there. Recall earlier in part one, I referenced evidence from the Heart Math institute that communicates there is validity to the coherence of heart energy?

Connect with your heart first and decide from there how it is you want to feel in your life. Hand on heart, sync yourself with the uniqueness of your heart's rhythms and desires. Let this help you gain a sense of what truly resonates for you, now at this moment. Use this as a tool to connect to your core desired feelings whenever you desire. Return to it during periods of transition or the beginning of a new year or new chapter.

Instead of being on a merry-go-round where your thoughts determine how you feel, and your feelings then influence what you do, become your own consciously loving leader. Decide to follow what feels really good, on a gut level. Your body never lies, remember. Your mind may deceive for a time, but your body always knows the truth.

Danielle Laporte is the champion of aligning your life according to your core desired feeling. She offers it to the world in such an empowering format. Here's a list of 20 core desired feelings. There are countless more to choose from of course. I want you to read through each of them. Hand on heart and notice which ones speak truth to you. Which ones resonate for you given the season you're currently in?

Decide how it is you want to feel in your one precious life.

RESILIENT	CHERISHED
LIGHT	CENTERED
FREE	ADVENTUROUS
STRONG	FIERCE
DEEP ROOTED	HARMONIOUS
DESERVING	LOVING
OPEN HEARTED	INSPIRED
JOYFUL	INTENTIONAL
TREASURED	BOUNDLESS
AUTHENTIC	CLEAR

What you are creating here, is an inner revolution. One where YOU become the architect of your present experience and the designer of your desired future. By attuning to how it is you really want to feel in your daily life, you begin to shift from past to present. From feeling powerless or like a victim to feeling powerful and inspired by life. From being a human doing to gaining real traction in your desired state of being. You become the architect, the designer of what is.

The process of coming to know, accept, and allow your core desires to show themselves to you, is also about taking a stand. Deciding how you want to feel, and then what you want to do about it. Whether it happens within the time frame that you want or even exactly how you want, matters less. What matters more here is that this becomes the framework that you creatively build your life upon. Again, and again return back to this.

How do I want to feel?
How do I want to feel in my home?
How do I want to feel in my most precious relationships?

How do I want to feel in my parenting?

How do I want to feel when I'm at work?

How do I want to feel when I look at myself in the mirror?

How do I want to feel when I reflect on my one precious life?

By asking and then bravely and courageously answering these questions, you are inviting deep soul-level healing to occur within. Even by asking these questions, you are changing the trajectory of your life.

What you're really doing here is bringing conscious awareness to aspects of yourself that have not received permission to be truly felt or acknowledged. You're giving voice to your desires. You're letting your uniquely divine feminine light begin to shine. You're expanding, no longer stuck or sinking, you're actively releasing greater potential into existence. You're doing what women for centuries before you (maybe even your own mother or grandmother) were never able to do for themselves. Courageously chart their own course.

Change is only change if we change

"When women lose themselves, the world loses its way. We do not need more selfless women. What we need right now are more women who have detoxed themselves so completely from the world's expectations that they are full of nothing but themselves. What we need are women who are full of themselves. A woman who is full of herself knows and trusts herself enough to say and do what must be done. She lets the rest burn." – Glennon Doyle, Untamed

There are many different theories that underpin how, when, and why people change. Instead of touching on many, I'm going to focus on one. The one I witness most often plays out when working with clients engaged in a transformational process alongside horses.

The reason why horses can be so valuable in the change process is that they encourage you to get OUT of your head, and INTO your body. It really is that simple, yet that profound.

The body never lies, remember. The body won't alert you to signs that it needs food, that energy is depleting, and hunger is approaching when it really isn't. The body won't inform you that there's a lump forming in your throat, a constriction that aches and feels difficult to get around if there really is no such thing occurring. Our bodies keep score. They are the truth-tellers. What we must do is learn to listen.

Horses help you get out of your mind, into your body, and closer to your heart. They are a gift to us from the natural world, at a time when we desperately need such gifts. As we explore these stages of change below, derived from the Equine Guided Education framework which was pioneered by the bold and brilliant Ariana Strozzi Mazzucchi, I encourage you to apply them to your own life.

There are four general stages of change I commonly witness people work through. As you read through them, consider where you are. Do you see yourself clearly in one stage, or possibly leaving one stage and entering into another? There is a flow to change that is dynamic and unique to each person. Practice leaning into a compassionate inquiry around what your change process looks like. Are you flowing through some aspects of these stages? Are you stuck in one stage unable to move beyond? Perhaps you don't see yourself reflected here, as you're pre-contemplative? The stage just before you accept and acknowledge that change is imminent or already occurring. Suspend judgment, invite curiosity.

The following four phases of change were developed by Ariana Strozzi Mazzucchi and are excerpted from her book, "Equine Guided Education."

Stage 1 ~ Identifying the place of change

- Acknowledge and accept that change is near, or already happening

- Get curious, invite a compassionate inquiry (where do you notice sensations in the body, repetitive thoughts in the mind, memories or images may emerge)

- Start with where you're at - locate the place or domain ready for change (is it personal, in your work life, or is it fundamental - meaning it affects everything)

- Notice if there are blocks or barriers. What might be inhibiting change to happen naturally?

Stage 2 ~ Explore and reflect

- Explore choices and possibilities

- Notice thought patterns, beliefs, and behaviors

- Distinguish between the 'old story' vs the 'new story'

- Decide on core desired feelings

- Reflect on values - begin to consider aligning values with actions

Stage 3 ~ Own, then tell your story

- Embody your experience - make it visceral and keep it in the present

- Speak about it with clarity and purpose to self and others, keep talking about it differently

- Practice moving your body, while honoring your new story. Visualize yourself doing it differently

- Allow confidence and resilience to develop naturally as you create this new story

Stage 4 ~ Take inspired new action

- Connect to your sense of self-agency (your fundamental will)

- Devote yourself to a few small new actions (opt for devotion overdetermination)

- Don't go it alone - be purposeful in inviting support and accountability

- Be fiercely gentle with yourself as you continually evolve

Anita's Walk with Horses

Here is a glimpse into the change process Anita went through. She rode a full feeling wave of compassionate curiosity that brought her to a place of deep remembering's in her relationship with her father. This embodied noticing created space for a horse to show up, offering her support in laying to rest what was historical and owning the story of what she now desired in her life.

Anita showed up for her first private session, exuberant and clad in cowgirl boots and a plaid jacket. As we walked into the first paddock to meet and greet the horses, Anita's presentation began to shift. She became less excited, increasingly quiet, and noticeably anxious.

As we walked through the gate together getting closer now to the horses, who were loose and free roaming in their paddock, Anita made a statement *"Are you sure the horses are ok with us coming in here? ...... I uh, think they might be annoyed that we're totally in their space."*

I paused, looked around at the horses, taking in their energy and observing the feedback they were providing as we entered into their space. Summer and Ginger were grazing at the hay feeders together, two other horses were grazing at the feeder on the far side and Gwen was standing at the far end of the paddock near the automatic water, just now noticing our entrance.

They hadn't moved much at this point, appearing to be occupied with their own agenda. I respond to Anita's question with a question *"What makes you think that the horses might not be OK with us in their paddock right now."*

"I'm not sure actually...It's just the first thing I wondered when we walked in." Anita replied.

"Ok. Well, this is what I'm curious about, why is it when you walk into this space, the first thing you verbalize is a sentiment around being welcome here... if you belong?" I inquire.

Anita paused while taking in the entirety of my question. *"Hmm, well guess I just realized, like just now, that in many situations this is how I show up.... with this automatic response, a questioning of if I'm welcome or wanted here...... uh oh wow, well that was big. Like this is a total story I've been telling myself for a long time, holy shit!"*

"For sure. How we do some things is quite often how we do many things. It can be really helpful to get curious about why that is and where it comes from. Ultimately it helps us heal it." I say to Anita.

I urge Anita, to stand down onto her feet, plant herself here for a moment and look around, notice, and take in each horse. I prompt her to get grounded and allow for a natural reflection to occur. Intentionally notice any sensations that feel like potential blocks or barriers she may encounter on this exploration.

Anita does just that. She rocks forward and back on her cowgirl boots then stands taller into herself. She draws a long breath in and a long slow exhale out. She begins to take in Summer and Ginger eating peacefully at the hay feeders. As Anita exhales Ginger looks over at her and mirrors her exhalation before returning to her lunch. Anita smiles and continues on with her gaze. She looks out at Gwen, who's resting by the water basin, head hung low, eyes half shut. Anita continues turning her head, now looking over at the two horses on the other side of the paddock. Both are peacefully standing together eating their lunch, tails swishing, the sound of chewing audible.

"Well just look at them… eating peacefully, relaxed, content. Giving zero fucks about me and my anxieties over here…. wow. That was a total reaction I just had, and the really interesting thing here is I totally know where that comes from. Like it's only certain situations that trigger a response like that. This is totally about my current relationship and likely the childhood relationship I have with my Dad. In both of those relationships, I struggle with feeling like I'm not really seen or chosen or valued. Like to some extent I have to hustle or always be earning it…Does that make any sense? Ugh, I was not expecting to feel this way with the horses." Anita disclosed.

"Feel what way?" I ask her.

"Well…. Insecure, weak, kind of sad, small, unimportant, and some shame mixed in there too" Anita offered.

"You sound clear in your naming of those feelings. Why do you feel that way now?" I ask her.

"I guess the reaction I had to first be in the horse's paddock reminded me of experiences I've had in the past - I felt a similar sense of insecurity, smallness, or vulnerability of sorts" Anita shares.

We stand together for the next 5 - 10 minutes in silence. Observing the horses, experiencing the emotions enlivened in the presence of the herd.

"I'm curious if you have a sense of how you do want to feel instead?" I wonder out loud to Anita.

"Do you mean how I want to feel right now? Or in relation to my dad and boyfriend," Anita asks.

I walk over beside Anita and stand close *"Either, both."* I say to her.

Anita begins to shuffle on the spot, shifting her weight from foot to foot, she clenches her hands together then releases them to her side. She takes another breath in, looks up at the sky, exhales slowly, and lets her gaze land on Ginger. She pauses here for a moment, shoulder to shoulder we stand, her eyes and energy fixed on Ginger.

I love this moment. I adore the pause before the shift. It's a tender moment in time that seems to slow right down before rising up and out. When a woman begins taking a stand for what it is she really desires. It sends a visceral vibration through my body. I wonder what it must feel like to the horses. Their innate sensing, much more potent and attuned than mine. I'm curious what it feels like to them to be in the presence of such vibrational energetic shifting.

Anita stands down into the ground and gets a little taller in her body - like she is inhabiting it more fully than she was just moments before. *"I want to feel solid, confident. I want to feel safe to be open-hearted....I don't want to question myself like I just did. I want to feel sure of myself inside and out.... secure in my own skin. I love me, I've got it goin' on."* She says slowly and more surely with every word. Like she is formulating each sentence from the center of her heart. Eyes on Ginger, words easily and effortlessly flowing out of her.

"Beautiful." I proclaim. "How about we practice exactly that then." I suggest.

I invite Anita to remain connected to the statement she just made about how she wants to feel. I ask her to begin embodying the feelings she desires; secure, confident, solid, open-hearted. I offer two suggestions to explore this. First, revisit a past experience where she felt this way, the first thought is usually the best thought. Alternatively, I invite her to create her own visualization or snapshot of what it feels like to feel openhearted, secure, solid within. Who is she with, where is she, what is she doing?

"So, what would it feel like in your body to feel the way you desire. Allow the visualization to encompass as much of yourself as you can.' I urge Anita to connect with her desired feeling state. Placing a hand on her belly and the other on her heart, begin to breathe. Allowing this feeling to rise up within her. To feel it in her belly, her chest, her heart. To allow it to rise up to her throat, to influence her speech, and to seep into her third eye, encompassing her thoughts.

"When you're ready, move towards a horse and make contact. Meet, greet, welcome a connection. Keep your core desired feelings at the forefront. I am right over here. Take your time." I invite her to move beyond the expression of words, and communication of feelings, inviting a deeper embodiment to occur. One where Anita gets to practice in the wise, generous company of horses, her desired way of being.

Halfway through our very first session together, Anita is at the fourth stage in this process of change. She arrived and walked into the horse paddock and realized straight off that change was underway. From the first interaction, she was able to identify the origin and moved quickly to a place of compassionate inquiry within herself. She then paused long enough to notice the patterns, why she felt this way, and with whom. She was able to distinguish that these thoughts, which determined her feelings, were based on an old historical story. One connected to her childhood relationship with her father, and the unsatisfying interactions with her subsequent male partnership. From here she was open to exploring the possibility.

After accepting and honoring her feelings, she became attuned to what her core desired feelings now are. She made a statement or declaration claiming this experience as her desired truth. She was then willing to practice moving forward, connected to her truth. Moving in the world towards her desires, owning and embodying confidence, moving each foot with purpose and solidarity. Approaching this new interaction from a place of open-hearted awareness, her sense of security increasing with every step and every breath.

Anita stood still before slowly but surely making a move. Step by step she walked closer to Ginger. Ginger looked up from her hay as Anita came closer. Anita stopped when Ginger looked up at her. They paused there together, taking each other in. Anita held her hand out to Ginger, offering a connection to this horse. Ginger picked her head up, intrigued she walked away from her feed to take a step towards Anita's outstretched hand. Anita softened visibly at this mutual expression of interest. Ginger sniffed Anita's hand then moved her muzzle up the length of her arm and paused for a moment, her large head now very close to Anita's chest, before moving her muzzle up Anita's face. Face to face they stood together. Anita allowing the curious intimacy of the moment to occur, softening into it with every passing second. Ginger welcomes the invitation to connect. She responds by moving into the space Anita created for this interaction to occur. Here they are together, building a connection infused with Anita's core desired feelings in mind.

"Her face is so soft and warm; her whiskers are tickling my chin. Oh my god, I can't believe she wants to be this close to me right now. I feel like I should move back and give her some space, but I SO don't want to… I want to just stay right here like this." Anita softens into the experience.

"Stay as long as you like. Allow yourself to be guided by your core, your center, not your thinking mind. If you feel unsafe or you've had enough, move. If you're enjoying it and you sense Ginger is a willing partner, stay and enjoy. Practice trusting your own knowing." I replied to Anita. *"Ginger will take care of herself. She will leave or move on, whenever she chooses to. If she stays and engages, it's because she wants to."*

These moments between Ginger and Anita are what confident, secure, and open-hearted exchanges look like. Anita can attest to what it feels like. My sense was receptive, curious, open, and willing. Relaxed, steady, and attuned to what's happening. Connected, inspired, warm-hearted bonding.

This is the first in a series of sessions Anita and I have together with the horses over a season. Time and again, she finds herself at various stages of this change process. Some experiences begin and conclude in one session, such as this. Other experiences begin and we revisit them several times in various ways with different horses throughout our time together.

Anita experiences several shifts throughout our coaching relationship. From feeling insecure, hustling for her worthiness, and being overly available to the needs of others in her life, to feeling deeply empowered. Confident in her ability to know what she wants and willing to practice trusting this budding confidence.

She transforms from feeling shame around her authentic desires to feeling free to explore these desires with a sense of clarity, compassion, and self-determination. She is lively, vivacious, bold, and the energy that exudes from her is that of a woman in love with herself. In love with her life and the possibilities that await her. She has this vibrant limitlessness about her energy that shines brightly and exudes warmth and genuine caring.

Her's was a story of a woman full of herself. The world does not benefit when women remain small, silent, or stuck in patterns of shame, anxiety, or fear. The world blossoms, when fully alive women claim what's rightly theirs. Their feminine divinity. Their authentic power. Their inherent freedom and vibrant spirit.

(Employing the Skyhorse EGE™)

Employing the Self - Other - World Perspective

Humans can have a felt sense and override it, horses on the other hand cannot. What comes up for them when interacting with you is something like this I imagine: "*Do I need to pay attention?*" and "*How present is she?*" as well as "*Can I trust her as part of the herd?*" and "*Does she really mean what she's asking?*"

Horses process information instinctually and emotionally. What determines their response to you comes from your way of being. Your energetic presence. How you hold and move your body, the tone of your voice, the odor you naturally emit. They trust their instinctual perceptions; they don't have the intellectual stories that humans do that cloud their perceptions. (Strozzi Mazzucchi, #173)

Few of us are able to accurately determine what it is that truly influences others. Maybe you think it's your intention, your logical thought, your authority. What it really is, however, is your BEingness. Your unique essence.

When we're centered and focused on what we care about, present yet flexible and open, horses know and will often engage or move towards. When we're off-centre, easily triggered, automatically reacting, having judgemental thoughts, horses also know and often will move away or opt not to engage. Horses react to inauthenticity. As social animals, their very survival is dependent on each individual's capacity to be responsible for themself. Inauthenticity communicates a level of distrust and a lack of safety.

I know you're familiar to some extent, with the relationship between mind - body - spirit. Horses invite a deeper layer of understanding here. They offer a bridge to the interconnectedness of all life. Inviting us beyond our current perspective of body-mind-spirit, to that of self- other- world.

In my ongoing mentorship with Ariana Strozzi Mazzucchi, equine guided educator and master somatic coach, I have gleaned these truths from working within this framework of understanding:

- "Your animal body is the self - it's where we hold all our memories and experiences. It's our first informant. Listen and trust your body's knowledge. In order to experience the changes occurring in your environment, you must first notice and then begin to shift the way your body responds to your environment.

- Your mind is connected to the other - it's how and what you think. How you relate to others and how others relate to you. Your mental interpretations often determine how you are perceived or how others perceive you. As social animals, you can't help but care about this. How healthy or unhealthy your self-perception is, is often directly related to how your mind is relating.

- Your spirit correlates with how you connect with your environment, the world at large. This includes your beliefs and values and fuels your purpose in the world. When you reconnect to your spiritual longings, you're increasingly more capable of changing and healing your relationship with the world, community, and family you live within."

This is where horses live. They invite you to access your spirit through imagination and curiosity, they invite you into the space of not knowing and not needing an answer. This invitation into the realm of feeling, sensing, noticing, and increasing your sensate awareness is how *they* can become *your* teacher.

To begin living from a self- other- world framework is to experience a whole new world of sensory awareness, it's where new insight and new interpretations are birthed. It's how you step off the merry-go-round of reaction and regret and begin to open to real and meaningful exchanges. This is how you'll be able to positively influence your loved ones, and ultimately have an impact on the kind of world your children (present or future) will be a part of.

Human Wisdom

How do our bodies do what they do and know what they know? Why is it that when the young sorrel horse Gwen approached me, I noticed myself stepping away? Yet when Summer, the old bay quarter horse mare came over for a sniff right after, I noticeably relaxed and moved towards her.

I'm no science geek, this is not where you'll find pages and pages on Polyvagal Theory or evidence that Somatic Processing is key in activating true healing and resetting overwhelmed nervous systems.

Instead, I'll briefly inform you on three areas of understanding, that are paramount to experiencing real healing and lasting change. Your Biology, your Psychology, and your Sociology. Simply put, ways to address healing in your body, ways to address healing your mind and behavior, ways to address healing your social connections and relationships.

Let's start with your body. Your *nervous system* influences nearly everything you do, think, say, or feel. It controls complicated processes like movement, thought, and memory. It also plays an essential role in the things your body does unconsciously, such as breathing, regulating your heart rate, how you respond to a rush of emotion, or when your guts indicate some activity is imminent.

Your nervous system affects pretty much every aspect of your health, including:

- Thoughts, memory, learning, and feelings.

- Movements, such as balance and coordination.

- Senses, including how your brain interprets what you see, hear, taste, touch, and feel.

- Sleep patterns

- Heartbeat and breathing patterns.

- Response to stressful situations.

- Digestion, as well as how hungry and thirsty you feel.

- Body processes, such as puberty and aging

This complex system is the command center for your body. It regulates your body's systems and determines how you experience yourself in your environment.

Let's go just a little deeper here, shall we? Your parasympathetic nervous system, also known as the rest and digest system is responsible for conserving energy, slowing down our automatic responses, and immobilizing you. This allows you to experience a state of recovery, increasing digestive functions and removing waste from the body. In this busy, high-stress, over-functioning world we exist in, cultivating a healthy parasympathetic nervous system often requires focused attention.

Your sympathetic nervous system is commonly known as the fight, flight, or freeze response. It mobilizes you by creating a boost of energy helping you to take action, move out of the way or respond with force. Your heart rate increases, and oxygen-rich blood flow elevates to help speed up your body's ability to function under imminent stress. You may know people who exist in this highly stressed state all the time.

By exploring your unique nervous system health in more detail you'll dive deeper into healing trauma and rewiring your brain through neural plasticity. What you'll really be doing is increasing your capacity to feel, process, and integrate your experience while remaining present and self-regulated.

If your nervous system is overwhelmed or under-functioning your experience of yourself, your loved ones, and the environment you live in is likely to suffer greatly. Simple somatic exercises can be highly beneficial in supporting the health of your nervous system so you can *mobilize* effectively or allow *immobilization* with ease while deepening *social connections* that support your inherently human need to bond with others.

Your body is your container. When you're able to regulate and heal your body, you heal your life.

Below are three somatic areas of practice that are often incorporated into the healing exploration horses inspire. These somatic tools can be greatly enhanced when partnering with horses who quite willingly seek to engage in such therapeutic processes. Horses are masterful at these 'techniques' as they're instrumental to their very way of being.

Grounding - Feeling your feet on the earth, your bum in the chair, your back on the sofa. Directing your attention to the sensation of support underneath and around you. There is a sense of feeling rooted that you are welcoming. You are also increasing your ability to stabilize yourself, body, mind, and spirit when you begin to focus on what types of grounding techniques feel good to you.

Orienting - Noticing if there is defensive or exploratory orienting occurring within? Through engaging all of your senses, can you explore where you are in time and space? What do you hear, what do you feel on your skin? Do you have a noticeable taste or texture in your mouth when you swallow? What do you see around you? Can you use descriptive words to shape your current experience? If you are one to get lost in your head or stuck in the mind, this can be a simple practice that will help to reorient you and bring you back into the present moment with ease.

Resourcing - Connecting with your container (your physical body, your energetic body, your spiritual body, and the energy around you) through self-soothing techniques. This can look like hands-on holding of self. Getting in touch with your physical container, a hand on your heart, and another on your belly. This may look like leaning into or standing very near a horse or that has offered itself to you in a therapeutic partnership. This can also include various ways of moving, breathing or connecting with the energy present in your body.

If this is fascinating to you, Dr. Peter Levine and Irene Lyon are nervous system specialists and neuroplasticity experts worth investigating. Irene has a wealth of easy-to-digest knowledge on the fascinating topic of healing your nervous system. She is my go-to gal when it comes to understanding and implementing simple exercises that can help heal trauma and create a greater capacity for self-regulation.

When you attend to the health of your nervous system, you begin to rewire your brain. This aids healing in your *biological* as well as your *psychological* self. When you learn how to self-soothe and regulate your emotions, then you are able to wholeheartedly engage with yourself and others from a place of safety.

Practicing recognizing the voice of your inner critic or self-saboteur is another way to cease energy going where it is not useful and begin to redirect it in a manner that is. This supports your psychological wellbeing and sets you up for greater mental stability. Resourcing yourself by getting the support you need, either within yourself or from another, is the path taken by those who seek healthy relationships and are willing to risk in order to gain connections. This supports healing your *sociology*, or social and relational connections.

From modern Neuroscience to ancient Eastern Philosophies. A blend of old-world healing philosophy and new age knowledge. Viewing your healing and health in terms of a bio-psycho-social lens (*your biology, your psychology and your sociology, as above*) can be useful in identifying what's going on where, and help you cultivate both willingness and action in order to experience healing.

Two ancient systems that inform your relationship with yourself, others, and the world, are the Koshas and the Chakras.

The koshas are essentially your subtle body. This system is made up of five sheaths or layers.

The first layer being your *physical body*. Your tangible physical structure and internal bodily systems. It is the densest and superficial of all five layers. You move, sense and experience, through your physical structure.

The second layer is the *energetic body*, it includes movement of chi, or prana - your life force. This layer makes your heartbeat, and your lungs breathe. This layer includes the seven main chakras, the nadis, and other energy channels within. You connect to your awareness and learn how to direct energy, by focussing on this layer.

The third layer is the *psycho-emotional body*. This layer includes your patterns of thought and emotion. It relates to your social roles, your personality, your emotional health. This layer includes your emotions and the connection between your thoughts and your emotions. Here is where your mind interacts with your past conclusions and beliefs to influence your perception of reality.

The fourth layer is the *wisdom body*. This is our inner intelligence, inner wisdom, or intuition. It is our power of judgment and inner discernment. It encompasses all of the functions of the higher mind. It discerns what is real and what is unreal. Tapping into this layer connects you to your innate wisdom.

The fifth and final layer is the *bliss body*. This is your true self, the center of your being. It feels like the pure joy that comes in moments of cherished silence or stillness. It is the state beyond words or actions, it is when we are connected to all that is. A sense of oneness and universal love.

Onto the Chakras. The Chakras encompass the seven main energy centers of the body. They correspond to the location of major endocrine glands and nerve centers. They run along the body's astral spine and are depicted as circular shape wheels of energy.

This ancient system was derived in India between 500 and 1500 BC. It originated from the oldest known text called the Vedas. The Chakras are how you can identify where energy is blocked or flowing freely and can provide you with key information, around the health and wellbeing of your subtle body system.

If you're already familiar with the Chakra system, skip on ahead. If not, here's a very brief overview of this ancient system of understanding and influencing energy works.

Root Chakra I AM. Located at the base of your spine, it is your foundation, your sense of support, your ability to ground. Its color is red, its element is Earth.

Sacral Chakra I FEEL. Located below your belly button and above your pubic bone. It is your connection to pleasure, creativity, emotions. Its color is orange. Its element is Water.

Solar Plexus Chakra I DO. Located below your heart and above your belly button, the center of your core. It is your power center, your sense of agency, your ability to act or initiate. Its color is yellow. Its element is Fire.

Heart Chakra I LOVE. Located in your chest, near your heart center. It is the area of unconditional love, love for self and others. Its color is green. Its element is Air.

Throat Chakra I SPEAK. Located at the base of the throat. It is your communication, your expression, and your purification. Its color is blue. Its element is Ether or Space.

Third Eye Chakra I KNOW. Located in between your two eyes, the center of the forehead. It is your perception, your inner command center, and your wisdom portal. Its color is purple. It is ALL of the elements.

Crown Chakra I UNDERSTAND. Located at the top of the head, the cerebral cortex. It is your universal consciousness, connection to all that is. Its color is white. Its element is space or bliss.

How you integrate and ultimately shift what is happening with your physical self, your energetic self, and your psycho-social self comes back around to where we started. Your stories, and the cyclical nature of all things. How your stories are affecting your daily experiences of yourself, how they influence your relationships, and how they'll either block or bless your future self.

Yes, there is value in exploring ways to further heal your nervous system. Indeed, tuning into your subtle body can help identify where and what is happening within. Certainly, balancing your chakra system is an excellent way to explore where you may be blocked or depleted or where you may be overwhelmed, with a surplus of energy.

How you can shift your experience right now and continually, is to practice something called *Cognitive Reframing.*

It's a fancy word for a simple psychological technique. It consists of identifying and then changing the way you speak about yourself, situations, experiences, events, ideas, and/or emotions. *Cognitive reframing* is how you challenge and then change old stories.

"Be impeccable with your word. Speak with integrity. Say only what you mean. Avoid using the word to speak against yourself or to gossip about others. Use the power of your word in the direction of truth and love." Don Miguel Ruiz. Author of the four agreements.

As far as we know, words and language have only been bestowed on humans. You and I are the only animals who use language as our primary source of understanding and being understood. So, it is language, the words we choose to curate our experience, that have the unique power to affect how we think, and shape how we feel and behave, now and as we move forwards.

Tina's Walk with Horses

Tina was participating in a small group healing retreat at the barn with seven others. After our group introduction and safety talk, we made our way over to the round pen, where Biscuit was waiting for us. Biscuit's horse-wisdom often reveals itself in her gentle, tender, kind-hearted, and a willing spirit. Tina was keen to volunteer for a turn in the round pen with Biscuit, or B (as she's often called).

Tina was given very basic instructions for this initial experience "Go in, allow yourself to land and ground somewhere first, then invite a connection to occur with Biscuit" I directed her.

Tina went into the round pen, as the other six participants stood just outside, witnessing her process while experiencing their own. I remained in the round pen with Tina, giving both her and Biscuit space to connect, while also observing the safety of the interaction and holding space for a deepening of awareness to occur.

Tina walked into the round pen and went right over towards Biscuit. Biscuit approached her and then quickly moved around so she was standing on Tina's opposing side. Tina moved over a few steps, noting the position both horse and human were now in, I made an assessment.

"Tina, I'm wondering what you notice about where you are right now" I prompted. Tina responded *"I'm close to her head, I like her. She feels calm and warm."*

"Ok, what I'm noticing is that you're also between the horse and the round pen rails. You have nowhere to go easily or quickly if you wanted or needed to. If she were to move quickly or unexpectedly, you'd potentially be in danger of getting physically hurt." I shared my observation and my concern about where she positioned herself.

Tina, looking around the round pen and then noticing where she was in relation to the horse in the space provided. She paused before saying *"This is what I do. I put myself in harm's way in order to gain connection"* Tears began to well at the corner of Tina's eyes, spilling out and onto her cheeks. *"I don't think I've realized how often I jeopardize my own safety in order to gain connection."*

I encouraged Tina to try again. To connect with what feeling safe alongside Biscuit might feel like and then move with focused thought and a desire to feel safe instead of in jeopardy as she'd mentioned. I encouraged her to tune into any and all sensations in her body.

Tina placed one hand on her belly then looked around and began to walk forward and around Biscuit's body. Finding a place close to the horse, yet with space to move more freely and the ability to notice what's happening all around her. Tina stopped moving, let her hands fall to her side, took a long deep breath in and out, then gazed upon Biscuit.

Biscuit held her gaze, exhaled, and then took a few steps towards Tina. She stopped with her head resting very near the center of Tina's body. She exhaled again and stood there for the duration of our session.

I inquired with Tina *"What are you noticing in and around your core right now Tina, where Biscuit's head is?"*

"I'm noticing a sense of warmth standing here with Biscuit so close to me. I feel like she's telling me something" she responded.

"Ok, let's explore that then" I suggest.

Tina looking into B's eyes, without looking up at me, nods her head yes.

"What might be the message behind the sensations you're feeling in and around your core" I gently probed. Tina paused, placed her hand on her belly before responding *"Well I feel very hollow. I have no connection to my core. No real sense of center."*

After waiting a few minutes together in stillness, I inquire *"Is there anything else?"*

"What I've been willing to do in order to get or keep connection.... with my ex, with my kids even, I act or do something without realizing that it's going against my and their best interest." Tina shared with us all.

"I'm noticing and remembering so many moments where I've felt like this before actually. Hollow and seeking".

"Do you have a sense of what you want to do with this feeling?" I ask her.

"Oh, I totally want to shift it or get rid of it. I know I don't want to continue to feel like this. That seems crazy to me." Tina replies.

"So, what do you desire then? How do you want to feel in this same situation?" I invite Tina to pause and consider if nothing is different except how she wants to feel and respond, what might that look like.

I support Tina in practicing reframing her narrative. *"Well, hmmm. I guess I could say something like I want to be more aware of my patterns, so I don't keep doing this same thing?"* Tina questions her attempt.

"Try again. Keep it in the present and make it positive, instead of focusing on what you're not doing." I instruct.

"Ok.... Uh, well I'm working on connecting with myself before taking action or making a choice. I'm committed to my own safety and wellbeing." Tina reframes her desire into a present tense declaration of what she is doing versus beating herself up by negatively holding onto what's already been done. This starts slow but gains momentum as she formulates a mantra that is aligned with her intent.

"Yes. Totally. That sounds clear and feels real to me in this moment" I validate her attempt at reframing. Biscuit leans into Tina's abdomen and begins to rub her head up and down as if she's scratching her third eye against Tina's solar plexus. *"Tell me what your experience is of Biscuit now. What does this feel like to you?"* I seek Tina's interpretation of this interaction between her and Biscuit.

"Awwwww" Tina softens and visibly melts. *"This feels so good. I feel like she's telling me, YES, it feels validating. My core feels more alive and responsive. I can actually feel it now. I know I need to strengthen myself here."*

Tina reached out her hand and placed it on B's forehead, kissed her third eye, then began walking towards the gate of the round pen.

Tina looked over to the group of six others and muffled a soft laugh *"Who's next?"* Some were leaning against the round pen taking in the experience, others wiping away a rogue tear brought on by the tenderness and transparency of Tina's experience.

All actively engaged by witnessing the unfolding of this exchange. I never really know what's going to happen in a group experience. How the women will respond to each other, and how the horses will respond to them. It's an exercise in trust and surrender. The awareness and healing that transpired throughout the remainder of the day rippled through each participant. Creating a symbiotic vibration of acceptance and collective connection making.

Practice

Journal Reflections

- Can you embrace the first law of healing today, exactly as you are now? Notice what comes up for you as you inquire.

- Are there aspects of your shadow self where you're withholding love and acceptance? Can you name them and begin the work of befriending these parts of yourself?

- Now that you're familiar with different ways to view the healing and change process, consider which aspects stood out to you?

- Once we begin to identify and remove the blocks to healing, healing often will naturally occur. What blocks may be present that are hindering your ability to naturally heal?

CHAPTER 7 – THE REMEDY OF CLARITY

"Tell me to what you pay attention, and I will tell you who you are" – Jose Ortega y Gasset

At some point in your life, you begin to get really clear on what you stand for, what's important to you, and what your foundation is made of or built upon. The process of getting clear will require you to strip away that which no longer feels true and begin to rebuild on a solid foundation of truth, acceptance, forgiveness, compassion, creativity, and love. A life built on other things will surely struggle to remain steady amidst life's storms.

This process, from chaotic and overwhelmed to peaceful and steadfast, from wounded and distrusting to secure and brave, from resentful and weary to forgiving and filled with compassion - doesn't just happen, unfortunately. You must go through a fire of sorts. Some call it an initiation or an attunement. A purging of what and who you are not, in order to re-discover the essence of who you truly are. You must return to the resilience of your inner girl, the one who played relentlessly, loved generously, protected fiercely, communicated freely, and existed innocently. Making peace with your child within is the foundation from which your adult self can flourish from.

Making peace with her may mean offering forgiveness or accepting forgiveness. It may mean releasing the anger, betrayal, and rage that you hold deeply and secretly within. Making peace with her may mean protecting her now like you couldn't protect her then. Consciously choosing who's welcome in your raft of belonging and knowing why that is. Making peace with her means freeing yourself of what was so that you can welcome what is to be.

After this fire, this purging of sorts, you will emerge more fireproof than you were before. You will own the skin you're in and learn how to love it unapologetically. You may feel raw, tender, and vulnerable. It's OK, this is simply you, unmasked. You'll practice being this raw, beautifully true version of yourself with others by putting up boundaries to protect the parts of yourself and your life, that are sacred to you. Sometimes it will be messy and feel complicated or awkward while other times it may flow and feel effortless.

This is the dance of coming home to yourself. Of honoring your past, living your present while consciously creating your future.

There is no way around this fire, except through it. Connecting with your divine feminine life force means no longer living a man-made linear one, ours is made up of circles. Like the seasons, birth, life, death, rebirth. This fire you'll go through, will not be your first, nor will it be your last.

How do you do this, what paths will lead you where your heart desires to go?

If you do what you've always done, you'll get what you've always got. In order to do power differently, you must liberate yourself from the old definition of power (that being power over or power above) to a more unified definition of power (that being power with and power among).

I've never loved the word power. I've struggled to feel powerful and have often found myself caught in a tangle with my ego over such language. What I've come to know over the years of dancing and dodging my relationship with power, is that for many women, power means peace. The kind of power I choose to explore, connect with and embody in my life now, is the kind of power that serves the greater whole. It's strong, potent yet isn't self-aggrandizing. The kind of power that enables freedom and peace and can change people's lives for the better. This kind of power comes with knowledge, wisdom, and a willingness to address your own healing. When women heal themselves, they heal families, communities, nations, and the world. One courageously powerful thought, feeling, action at a time.

Rhonda's Walk with Horses

Rhonda began taking riding lessons a little over a year ago. She rode as a girl and was keen to get back in the saddle, literally. She craved something for herself, someplace she could go and some activity she could involve herself in that brought her joy and connection outside of her roles as mother, wife, daughter, sister, and business owner. Despite loving those roles, they often exhausted her. She carried much of the familial burden, as women do, and felt a building resentment rising within her.

She began to ride Aloe. Often lazy, Aloe provided her safety from which to reconnect with her riding body, while establishing what the connection with her inner will felt like. Rhonda began internalizing what she really wanted. Our work together determined how she was going to ask Aloe to partner with her, in order to achieve it.

As their bond built slowly over the weeks and months, they moved from a walk to trot, bending and turning, softening and strengthening with ease and grace. Soon they were ready to move from trot to canter. The transition from trot to canter happened, as it does with less ease and grace. Like in life; when things get fast, they can also get messy.

Every time they found their balance and rhythm together at a trot, and the next step was to transition into a canter, Rhonda lost her flow and would resort to asking Aloe to walk. Aloe, responding to the conflict she felt within her rider and provided Rhonda feedback amidst the transition.

"What do you notice happening right at the moment you're going to shift from trot to canter?" I inquire. *"Well, I slide my outer leg back and make contact with her side, she feels this, and I feel her kind of amp up some from behind, then I hold my reins tighter, and then Aloe shakes her head and neck, and then I slow down to walk, that's what I notice. I know I'm blocking her with my reins, or maybe my seat... I'm not sure why. I guess, if I'm honest she scares me a little bit."* Rhonda discloses.

"This is so helpful; you already have so much insight. Ok, let's dig into it some more." I reply. *"So, what are the thoughts that are coming into your mind as you think canter and your body prepares to ask for the canter?"* I ask. Rhonda pauses before answering, *"I'm thinking, what if I can't stay on through the transition, what if she bucks me off. Her power as she speeds up really throws me off. I feel like I'm not sure I can handle it."* Rhonda shares.

"Ok, so what I hear you saying, is that there's something about her power and remaining balanced and stable atop such power, that feels challenging for you or creates a fear response?" I check back in with her. *"Yes. Exactly"* Says Rhonda.

"So, this is what I'm noticing from where I stand …. When you get to the precipice, and you're ready, able, and almost willing to shift gears, Aloe is with you. She is right there with you. Your connection is mutual. She's listening and responding to you. What it looks like, is that you're blocked when it comes to consciously moving the power through your body. Instead of noticing the resistance within, breathing through it, and carrying on, trusting your connection and abilities, you quit. The head and neck shake you're getting at that moment from Aloe, looks like excitement or anticipation, maybe frustration even. Essentially it's feedback for you about what's happening in your partnership at that moment" I offer Rhonda my assessment.

"Yup, you're right. I'm stuck at that point of power. I take hold of the reins, she shakes her head, feeling the energy rise and anticipating it, I get scared and doubt myself and her, and then I shut the whole thing down. Geez, why do I do that? I never used to feel nervous or worried about picking up a canter?" Says Rhonda.

"Let's run through a visualization exercise before trying it again. Close your eyes for a moment, imagine yourself trotting around the circle to your left. You've got contact on the reins; you can feel her face through your fingers. Your hands are soft but attentive, when she softens her face and brings her head down slightly, you respond in kind by softening the grip on your reins the same amount. You have a reciprocal conversation going right now through your whole body. You're breathing in tune with her movement, it's easy, relaxed, you're enjoying the flow with her. You decide when you get just past the mounting block, you're going to ask her to canter. You look towards the mounting block, sit down onto her back, slide your leg back slightly and then kiss to her. She hears and feels this request and you feel a surge of power from her hind end, moving forward, you love this surge of power. It's exhilarating and makes you feel alive. Aloe shakes her head in anticipation and excitement over the movement and begins to canter. You are moving together beautifully. Like big rolling waves, you effortlessly cover the ground together. Breathing and moving with ease and grace. After two or three laps, you smile and allow your energy to lighten. Aloe feels the shift and responds by trotting. She exhales three long, loud breaths. You literally laugh out loud, feeling empowered and so fully alive. You break down to a walk, run your hand down her mane and come to a stop at the center." I finished the visualization and Rhonda opens her eyes and offers an emphatic *"YES! Let's do it."*

And just like that, she does. Just as we co-created together, moments before, Rhonda made manifest exactly what she pictured as her desired reality and succeeded in bringing it to life.

What you pay attention to defines who you are. When you focus on your perceived lack, your unfounded fears, and your low-lying anxieties, they become amplified in your life. When you focus on the space between where you are, and where you want to be, you're instead filled with creative possibility.

I've paid an erroneous amount of attention to the size and shape of my body. For years, it defined who I was, how I felt, who I interacted with and why. I've paid attention to God, how he and my early religious indoctrination was imposed on me. It determined how little joy I experienced and how much shame I carried around. I've paid attention to men. They defined how I felt about myself in their presence and how much I had to shrink in order to not threaten or disrupt their status quo. I've paid attention to my children. They have helped me define what learning to love throughout a lifetime really looks like. I've paid attention to horses. Horses have helped me internalize what real-life grace, power, and beauty look and feel like to me. They've also revealed how creatively we can travel our unique healing paths. I've paid attention to nature. The preciousness of our natural world inspires a sense of humbly and creatively living within it.

Belinda's Walk with Horses

Belinda is a brilliant and big hearted fifty-something professor. She responded to an invitation to join a wild, wise and free retreat I was co-hosting in the interior of BC's ranch country. She's warm, intelligent, delightful. There was a noticeable sense of repression or holding back with Belinda. A sense that she was here for something, she just didn't know what just yet. She participated in all of the offerings throughout this three-day intensive experience. It was her instantaneous connection with the horses, that captivated me and piqued a deeper interest in her attendance. She lit up when in their presence. There was a lightness and vibrancy present when witnessing her interactions with the herd.

On the second day of our retreat, we explored mounted movement and restorative practice with Summer, one of the horses selected as an ally for this group of ten ladies.

When it was Belinda's turn, it took her some time and support, orienting herself from the ground to finding stability while mounted on Summer's back. With every step Summer took, Belinda wobbled. Gripping with her legs, holding tightly with her hands while teetering on her crotch. It took Belinda some time to find center within her body and relax into the rhythm of Summer's four-beat walk. She became acquainted with horse time. Where everything slows to about quarter time. The four-beat rhythm syncing with the breath, and the reactions of the mind begin to diminish into a quiet spaciousness.

Belinda began to transform. Her rigid muscles began to soften and find a natural balance atop Summer's gently sloped back. As Summer's head lowered and her gait elongated, Belinda's spine lengthened, her hips opened, and she wrapped herself around the barrel of this horse. Moving together effortlessly and with ease.

Belinda softened her grip, taking her hands off of the large, round surcingle handles, designed to steady and support. She rode with her arms hanging freely at her sides, hips swaying with the movement, legs gently connected to Summer's side body and eyes wide and wild, looking longingly between the ears of this horse. Belinda looked over at me, holding the lunge line at the center of this large circle we were creating together. This sacred circle, where Belinda's tension and anxiety melted away before our eyes.

She was transforming into this wilder, wiser, and free-er version of herself. As she looked at me, she asked "*Has anyone ever had an orgasm while doing this? Hoo Wee…. I could totally see how that could happen…."* Belinda exulted. Exposing this sliver of unabashed delight with us all.

Summer, responding to Belinda's authentic expression, begins to speed up. Transitioning from her steady and relaxed four-beat gait, to a jog or two-beat trot. Belinda returns her hands to the handles and re-establishes balance at this new speed.

"Is this pace ok for you Belinda?" I inquire. Seeking affirmation that indeed she is loving the power and pace of what she's experiencing right now.

"Yeehaw !!" Belinda exclaimed. *"Hahaha haha, I don't even care how this looks, I am LOVING how it feels!"*

I urge Belinda on "Belinda, tune into your root, your backbone. Connect your backbone with Summer's backbone. Feel the support she's providing you, even as you navigate this heightened energy."

Belinda beams. She finds a connection through rounding her tail bone, lifting her pubic bone, and grounding herself in the movement. Her focus is palpable. She is a determined woman. She again lets go with her hands, remaining here for a few more laps, bouncing around atop Summer's back. Wobbling for a second, then finding her groove again. Her focus is pure, her presence potent.

Summer speeds up again. As her trot gets faster, it gets increasingly bumpy. Making it difficult for Belinda to ride this wave of movement without holding on or bouncing around.

I slow Summer to a walk, and check-in with Belinda *"I'm wondering if you'd like to canter. To transition from the speed you were just at, to what Summer is offering you next?"*

Belinda looks down at Summer. Leans forward and runs her hand lovingly along her dark mane. She looks over to me. *"Do you think I should?"* Belinda asks with the innocence of a young girl.

"Belinda…. Do YOU want to? Suspend the mind for a moment, does your body and spirit want to give it a go?" I reply.

"HELL YES! I'm going to try," Belinda exclaimed.

I offer some coaching to Belinda around how she can ask Summer to transition from trot to canter smoothly. I let her know she can remain in canter for as long as she likes. Summer has permission to slow down or stop when she chooses. I coach Belinda on how to ask her to slow down when she's ready.

Belinda adjusts herself on Summer's back, taking a few moments to focus and ground herself before embarking on this next adventure with this horse. She inhales, exhales, and then she is off. Belinda hoots and hollers, hair flying wildly in the wind. Summer speeds up the canter and lets out a loud exhale. Belinda bounces around, before returning to the focus and presence she'd cultivated earlier with Summer.

Within a few laps, she finds a steady seat. Her hips moving creatively in sync with Summer's movement. She lets go with her hands; Summer slows her canter to an easy cruising speed. They travel like this together for five or six laps before quickly transitioning back down to a walk. Belinda returns her hands to the handles as Summer slows her pace, and leans forward, draping her body over the surcingle handles and onto Summer's neck in an awkward-looking hug. They walk together like this for a lap. Wild woman and free horse. Bonded together by reciprocal energy. Unified movement, and deep listening.

Summer comes to a stop. She looks over and begins to walk towards me, indicating that she is done. This portion of the experience is complete. Before Belinda dismounts off Summer's back, we shift from movement into stillness. Exploring restoration with the support of Summer. Belinda wraps her legs over the handle of the surcingle and stretches herself down onto Summers' back. She is draped over the horse like a towel hanging on a rail to dry. Lifeless, soft, and supported by the steadiness of Summer's body.

As Belinda followed along with my verbal guidance to tap into the layers of her subtle body, shifting from her mind by way of attuning to her breath, she began to have a visceral response to the energy moving within her. She began to shake; her body began to clench and writhe atop Summer's body. Summer stood still. Supporting Belinda and honoring her experience by standing steady amidst the fluctuating energy. Belinda moaned and then cried out. She was both there and elsewhere at the same time. I placed my hands on Belinda's feet, pressing into her in order to maintain a sense of grounding and connection while she processed what was moving up and out of her.

This was old trauma, making its way out of the body.

Belinda allowed the experience to run its course and soon returned back to a sitting position atop Summer's back. She slid off the side of Summer, walked up to her face, and kissed her on her forehead. Belinda is noticeably shaken. The intensity and diversity of her experience with Summer linger in the air. We hug. We stand together for a moment. There are no words, just feelings, just energy. This sense of profundity and power lingering. To describe this experience with language feels like shortchanging the potency of it somehow. Her's was a full body healing experience.

Belinda walks over to the gate, where the other women are waiting, witnessing. They open the gate and Belinda walks out, noticeably different than how she walked in.

When you live in your head, disconnected from the wisdom of your body and the warmth of your heart, you suffer. When you make space for trauma and historical pain to be processed and transmuted, that is what can happen. When you follow what resonates, when you pursue inspiration, you connect with your truest self and your highest vibration, you experience vitality and aliveness. When you do what you are told, when you follow what's been taught or expected without thought or self-inquiry, you will remain stuck in patterns of shame, anxiety, and fear of rejection.

When women stop focusing on the pleasing of others, they will finally be free to please themselves.

The world desperately needs mothers, daughters, sisters, leaders, partners, and friends, who are free to please themselves.

This is the magic of communing with horses. Although they are domesticated, mostly living within human-made structures that contain their bodies, they remain free spirits. Their existence is one where they live only in the now, while in a relationship with themselves, each other, and their environment. They are true to themselves while being thoughtful of each other. They think neither in terms of past nor future, but remain fully connected to all that is, in this present moment. When horses are healthy, thriving, living in herds together, this is their true nature. Like humans however, when they are isolated, lack adequate connection, movement, and nourishment, they too suffer. Their spirit diminishes and their body pays the price.

They eat when they feel hungry, drink when thirsty, rest when tired, play when frisky, connect when curious or seeking, and express exactly what they're feeling or experiencing authentically at any given moment. They are our modern-day idols, as they represent what living a wild, wise, and free life, can look like.

You become like the company you keep. Tell me what you pay attention to and I will tell you who you are.

People, Places, and Process

"Do the difficult things while they are easy and do the great things while they are small. A journey of a thousand miles must begin with a single step." – Lao Tzu.

It might feel like where you're at feels very far from where you'd like to be. That's ok, know you're exactly where you're meant to be right now. Nothing needs to be different in order for you to do whatever small, great thing that will bring you closer to your own divinity. We are all just walking each other home after all. We are all journeyers on a shared path.

Yes, if inspired you could choose to spend some time in the company of horses. By now, you have a greatly expanded sense of who they are and how they may be a blessing to you in your life. Sure, you can sign up for a week-end retreat. Immersing yourself in an experience designed to rejuvenate you, reconnect you, and inspire your replenishing. Absolutely, you can find a coach, therapist, mentor, or shaman. One who sees you guides you and supports both your unbecoming and your becoming. One who is an ally for you as you travel the roads your heart directs you to. One who honors who you are and where you're at, while actively encouraging you to stay the course and transcend your perceived limitations.

You can read books, take online classes, meditate, practice yoga, and other embodiment methods.

All of it is good. Useful. Divine even. What healing, growth, and the ongoing development of your beautiful self-boils down to - is knowing that you're worthy of all it and accepting that you alone are in the driver's seat of your life.

None of it will do for you - what your heart is not yet ready for. You choose your people. You choose your time and place. The horses, the coaching, and the courses you take will not do for you, what you are not yet ready for. Universal timing is perfect. It guides you towards what you need when you need it. Your job is to pay attention and follow it. Rely on resonance. There are countless valuable tools, resources, and processes out there that are available to you. Follow what resonates. There are many ways to get from here to there.

There's a big value for every single one of us in Step 4 of the Alcoholics Anonymous 12 step program.

Step 4: Make a searching and fearless moral inventory of yourself.

This is a critical step. One we want to rush past. Driven by the desire for results, we often miss this key piece. Taking an honest inventory of where you are, why you're here, and what needs to shift. This step saves you energy, time, and money in the long run. It's the design that comes before the architecture. The planning, before the building.

There is an unlimited number of programs, processes, and paths you can take that will set you up to do the work of healing your wounds and living an aligned life. One that corresponds with your evolving values and beliefs. When you live out of integrity with yourself, at some point you will come to know this truth. Our bodies don't lie after all. There's only so long you can carry on as is before you pay a price for doing so.

This process below is the one presented to me by the horses. The one that humans who walk with horse's experience in some way shape or form, again and again. Here, I have taken the wisdom of the natural world and infused it with some modern-day positive psychology, nervous system insight, cognitive-behavioral techniques, and somatic awareness principles. It's a fusion of horse wisdom and spiritual practice.

It's clear and it's kind. It's a place to start when you're ready and willing.

The C.L.E.A.R. is kind process
~ to gain clarity and access healing.

This easy-to-digest inner exploration will help you harness the energy of your masculine while remaining connected to your feminine. You do not need to trade one for the other. Both aspects and energies are useful here. Both stillness and movement. Both intuitive and goal oriented. Both responsive and strategic. Both curious and logical.

Be willing to contract in order to be able to expand.

This can be a challenging truth to accept. Humanity is changing and expanding at such a rapid rate. To only seek expansion, without honoring the associated contraction is like occupying the light, yet never engaging with the dark. Or always moving, never resting. Always giving, never receiving. One cannot be sustained, without the other.

When we engage the subtle body with a sense of compassion, patience, and kindness - we reap the fruit of such interactions. First within yourself, then with precious others.

Let's go through this process together. Notice what you notice. Suspend judgment and open into a compassionate inquiry with yourself. Give yourself permission to allow what is, to surface naturally and with ease. I will guide you every step of the way.

It's helpful to have a journal or notepad/pen handy to jot things down as they arise. Find somewhere you can sit, rest, pause and become still. First the stillness, then the knowing.

Get quiet with yourself. Allow yourself 10 - 15 minutes minimum to experience and explore.

From this place of stillness, intentionally invite a sense of calm.

C - CALM   Cultivate an intentional, open-hearted peaceful state.

- Here you are becoming grounded, mindful, attentive to what's beneath the surface

- Feel the earth, floor, seat beneath you. Orient yourself to your space

- Close your eyes and begin to shift your attention inward

- Begin to contract and expand, through your breath

- Place a hand on your belly, and first breathe all the air out, CONTRACT.

- Begin to inhale, EXPAND and then exhale CONTRACT in your own natural rhythm.

- Stay here for 10 full breathes, or 1-2 minutes

- Invite a mindful presence. When your mind becomes busy, return your attention to your breath. Suspend judgment, opt for curiosity.

L- LEARN   Notice all sensation, tension, or restriction in the body.

- This is the Energy Diffusion Technique: *(BREATHE- RELAX- FEEL-WATCH- ALLOW)*

- Through a conscious reflection valuable insight can be yielded

- The physical and energetic body provides you a roadmap to explore

- Pause here and write down what and where you notice the sensation. Being specific and detailed helps

- You're opening into an inquiry. Your giving permission for sensation and emotions attached to sensation, to be felt and acknowledged.

- Remember, feelings are for feeling. Allow them to come and then to go. No need to attach, just notice

E- EXPERIENCE   Own and name your experience.

- Speak, Write, Draw or creatively emote your experience

- Identify the sensations, get curious about the feelings behind the sensations. Can you name them?

- Examine what's been your experience with what arose?

- Do you have stories around this that are ready to be unpacked or further examined?

- What is it like for you to simply attend to them, with curiosity and compassion?

A - ACTION The small but specific actions you will take on behalf of your own healing/growth

- Can you let something go, surrender something, or resource yourself in some way that will support you?

- Connect to your heart energy to guide your action steps. Place your hand on your heart and pause. Notice what comes up first, before engaging your thought process

- You are cultivating a mindful response.

- Know your Yang (what your masculine energy looks/feels like, how you can engage it purposefully) Keep to the Yin (return to your feminine essence, reside and renew here)

5. R - REAUTHOR Rewire your thought and behavior patterns - *Cognitively Reframe*

- Start by being impeccable with your word. Do not use your words to speak against yourself or others.

- Be intentional and positive in how you choose to put language into your experience. Your language shapes your reality.

- Consistency is Key. Keep showing up for yourself through ongoing intentional practice.

- Fix mistakes when you make them. Don't wait, correct your language ASAP

Remember this is a process you implement over and over again to gain clarity, invite healing and move on from what was and invite what is. It takes time for the body to relax and feel. It won't happen in 30 seconds, give your nervous system at least three minutes minimum to adapt to this slower pace. The process of resting and digesting is one you must create for yourself frequently in order to reap the benefits and reset a chaotic or traumatized nervous system.

No one wants to have the same arguments, work on the same issues, or repeat patterns again and again. How boring and absolutely frustrating. This process will not guarantee you a conflict or stress-free life, it will however provide the tools needed to navigate conflict and discern the root of stress. By practicing this process as often as you can, it becomes less like something you DO and more a part of who you are and how you respond. You integrate it into yourself. Becoming mindful in the present and then mindful in your response is the art of peace-filled living. This alone will save you from bouts of anxiety, resentment-fueled interactions, and sleepless nights.

Here's a quick recap on getting *Clear,* while being *kind* to yourself. Ground & center yourself using your breathing. Contract and expand naturally. Soften to what is, then notice what comes up. Lean into the learning. What has/is your experience been with what arose - inquire with compassion and name it. Where and how can you take gracious, loving action on your own behalf? Begin to tell a new story, start by being intentional with your speech. Apply the first law of healing ~ how can you consistently practice loving what it is you care about through this process.

Consider where and who you were when you began reading about *Women Who Walk with Horses.* Did you have hopes or dreams about what you would discover amidst these pages? I sense there's healing, growth, and expansion that's occurred for you on some level already. Although our journeys may differ, we are traveling similar paths. One where authenticity, freedom and peace lead the way.

When lost, as undoubtedly you and I will be again and again, pretty much forever, let us instinctively know to return home. To our own divinity. Home within ourselves. To the connections we've made with the natural world. To our own uniquely precious selves, and to each other.

Practice

Journal Reflections

- What are you paying attention to and how is that defining who you are?

- Do you feel like what you pay attention to is an accurate reflection of your present values?

- What is an example in your own life, where you've had to contract in order to be able to expand?

- What stood out for you in the C.L.E.A.R process of healing?

- Consider what you've engaged in, in the spirit of healing? Have you followed what resonates for you or have you followed what's expected of you?

CHAPTER 8 –
BRAVE NEW ENDINGS

"There will come a time when you believe everything is finished. That will be the beginning." Louis L'Amour

One of the purest joys a life with horses offers is witnessing the moment when horses, after being stalled or penned up for a time, finally get access to space, pasture, or grassy lands. This site never fails to send a visceral shot of joy right to the heart. There's this moment when the paddock gate opens or the trailer door swings wide, and a new reality is upon them. One that offers them room to move without restraint. If you've yet to witness such a moment, let me tell you, it is magnificent!

Often in a single step, a horse will move from containment to freedom. Once this gate or threshold opens, they become the embodiment of freedom. Horses will run, buck, fart, twist, hop, and bolt in one direction then switch gears in a single stride and jet off in the opposite direction. Heads high, tails in the air, they'll prance about as if they've just won the most coveted prize... they have after all. The gift of Freedom.

Let us not waste what is rightly ours. Peace. Freedom. Authenticity. Joy and Love.

These blessings are not bestowed upon all of humanity after all. Many of us still suffer living lives bound by obligations to another. We lack the freedom to wear, speak or behave however we choose. We are limited by religious confines, cultural mandates, economic or racial inequalities. Where joy is muted. Where the ability to give and receive love freely and easily is diminished.

It is a waste to not fully live the life you've been given. To hide from, numb or avoid what speaks to your unique heart and soul. To allow your challenges, real or perceived to block the remedies that await you. The best teachers on this journey will show you where to look, but they won't tell you what to see. The seeing belongs to you. The seeing and the knowing are yours alone.

What you do from here, whether you decide to begin removing the barriers between the life you have and the life you desire to create for yourself, comes down to you. It always does. Is committing to healing over holding on worth the reward? Is giving up the old story so you can finally create one that belongs to you first and foremost worthwhile? It all comes down to a willingness to face our fear and the cultivating the support needed to do so. Birth, life, death, rebirth.

Our fear after all isn't that we are inadequate. It's in fact that we are powerful beyond measure.

As Marianne Williamson famously reminds us "Our deepest fear is not that we are inadequate. Our deepest fear is that we are powerful beyond measure. It is our light, not our darkness that frightens us. We ask ourselves, who am I to be brilliant, gorgeous, talented, fabulous? Actually, who are you not to be? You are a child of God. Your playing small does not serve the world. There is nothing enlightened about shrinking so that other people won't feel insecure around you. We are all meant to shine as children do. We were born to make manifest the glory of God that is within us. It's not just in some of us; it's in everyone. And as we let our own light shine, we unconsciously give others permission to do the same. As we are liberated from our own fear, our presence automatically liberates others."

I hope this walk with horses has above all else, connected you more deeply with yourself. May you be inspired to do whatever small great thing possible, to bring about greater Peace, Freedom, Joy, and Love. To make manifest within you that which is ready to be birthed. My sister, it has been a delight.

Blessings.
Tracy & the Horses

BIBLIOGRAPHY

1. The Body Keeps Score, Bessel A. van der Kolk, M.D. Penguin Books, 2014

2. Kilby, Emily R. "The demographics of the US equine population." humanesociety.org, 2007. URL-https://www.humanesociety.org/sites/default/files/archive/assets/pdfs/hsp/soaiv_07_ch10.pdf

3. https://www.humanesociety.org/sites/default/files/archive/assets/pdfs/hsp/soaiv_07_ch10.pdf. Accessed 05 02 2021.

4. Middle Childhood. CDC center for disease control and prevention, https://www.cdc.gov/ncbddd/childdevelopment/positiveparenting/middle.html.

5. Hannah Ritchie (2019) – "Gender Ratio". Published online at OurWorldInData.org. Retrieved from: 'https://ourworldindata.org/gender-ratio' [Online Resource]

6. Napikoski, Linda. "Patriarchal Society According to Feminism." ThoughtCo, Feb. 11, 2021, thoughtco.com/patriarchal-society-feminism-definition-3528978.

7. Estés, Clarissa Pinkola. Women Who Run with the Wolves: Myths and Stories of the Wild Woman Archetype. New York :Ballantine Books, 1992

8. Kohanov, Linda (2001). The Tao of Equus: a woman's journey of healing & transformation through the way of the horse. Novato, CA: New World Library.

9. Strozzi Mazzucchi, Ariana. (2015) Equine Guided Education. Horses healing humans healing earth. Middletown, DE.

10. Grandin, Temple, and Johnson, Catherine. Animals in Translation. New York: Scriber, 2005.

11. https://www.taoofhorsemanship.com/heart-math Best, Caroline. The Tao of horsemanship. 2021.

12. McLean, Lee. Horsewoman. Notes on living Well and Riding Better. Red Barn Books. 2019.

ABOUT THE AUTHOR

Tracy fell in love with the magic of horses at the early age of 5 on her Grandparents farm. Her connection to farming and ranch life manifested during her early 20's when she married a cowboy. Together their family operated a 300- acre working horse and cattle ranch in BC's Cariboo country. An innate affinity for wide open spaces and animals living in harmony with each other and the earth, Tracy was immersed in the breeding, training, selling and management of her family's herd of 100+ horses.

As a western rider, therapeutic riding instructor, equestrian vaulting coach, and equine guided educator, Tracy's coaching and training has shape-shifted throughout her 23 years in the equine industry. As a single mother for much of her life, Tracy navigated her passion for horses, while counselling and educating children, youth and families who experienced crisis, developmental challenges, family trauma, disordered learning, as well as social - emotional difficulties. These experiences inspired Tracy to look beyond the traditional ways of teaching and guiding to a more holistic and engaging way to build connection and inspire real change. Ranch life inspired a spiritual awakening. The call to live close to the land, in harmony with mother earth and the animals in her care, fuels her passion for helping heal both horses and humans. Tracy is a long-time Sunshine Coaster, who along with her husband Darren spend time on the Sunshine Coast of BC as well on their land, Gray-Star Farms in Penticton BC.

Made in the USA
Las Vegas, NV
18 September 2021